NEW HAMPSHIRE
Our Home

Julie Baker

GIBBS SMITH EDUCATION
TO ENRICH AND INSPIRE HUMANKIND

To the children of
New Hampshire

First Edition
© 2010 Gibbs Smith Education

19 18 17 16 15 14 13 12 11 10   1 2 3 4 5

Published by Gibbs Smith Education
PO Box 667
Layton, UT 84041
801.544.9800
www.gibbs-smith.com/education

Project Editors: Jennifer Petersen and Hollie Keith
Editorial Assistants: Charlene Reyes and Linda Nimori
Photo Editors: Janis Hansen and Kris Brunson
Cover and Book Design: Jeremy C. Munns

Front cover photo credits: upper left, Debra Pero; lower right, Library of Congress
Back cover photo credits: Shutterstock

Gibbs Smith books are printed on either recycled, 100% post-consumer waste, FSC-certified papers,
or on paper produced from a 100% certified sustainable forest/controlled wood source.

Printed and bound in China
ISBN-13: 978-1-4236-0019-0
ISBN-10: 1-4236-0019-3

ABOUT THE AUTHOR

JULIE BAKER received her BA in anthropology and history from the University of Texas and her MEd from Boston College. A resident of New Hampshire for more than two decades, Ms. Baker has come to love the history and culture of the Granite State and especially enjoys learning about 19th-century New Englanders who helped shape American society.

Ms. Baker is the award-winning author of *The Bread and Roses Strike of 1912* and *The Great Whaleship Disaster of 1871*. Her articles have appeared in *American History* magazine and several academic presses, and she is a frequent lecturer at writers' workshops and teachers' conferences. When she's not researching or writing about people and places of the past, Ms. Baker works as an adjunct professor of English at Daniel Webster College in Nashua and Southern New Hampshire University in Manchester. She lives in Amherst with her husband and two daughters.

ABOUT THE RESEARCHERS AND CONTRIBUTORS

JESSICA ELLIS teaches and writes about teaching in Concord, New Hampshire. She has worked in education for over five years and looks forward to a long career in the classroom.

KARRY GAY is a fourth-grade teacher at Chichester Central School in Chichester. She has taught for 10 years and has a teaching certification in K–8. She lives in Loudon with her husband and two children.

KENNETH RELIHAN has been the Social Studies Consultant at the New Hampshire Department of Education since 2001. Prior to that, he taught high school history and government for 28 years. A New Hampshire native, he graduated from Nashua High School and the University of New Hampshire. He resides in Alstead, nestled between the Monadnock Region and the Connecticut Valley.

AUDREY ROGERS has a BA in History from Tufts University, an MA in History from the University of NH/Durham, and an MA in Curriculum and Instruction with a minor in Economic Education from the University of Massachusetts/Lowell. She is an assistant professor in the School of Education at Southern New Hampshire University, and she is an educational consultant and recent past president of the New Hampshire Council for Social Studies. Ms. Rogers is certified in grades 5 through 12 in social studies and taught at Nashua High School from 1989 to 2001. She has written several Jackdaw Primary Source Kits and coauthored *Cooperative Learning Basics* with Robyn Griswold. She was chosen New Hampshire Social Studies Teacher of the Year in 1997.

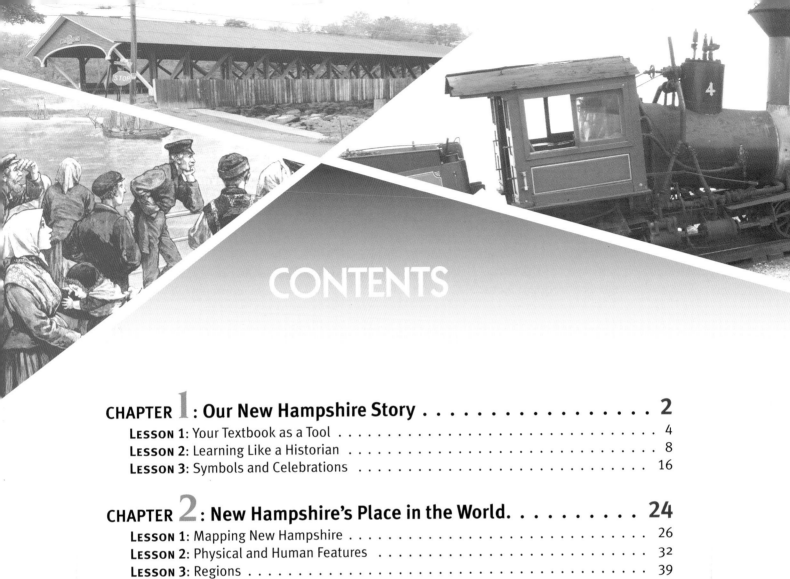

CONTENTS

REFERENCE

MAPS

INSPIRATIONS

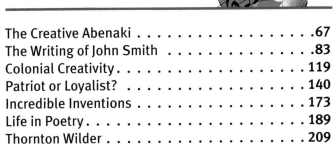

SPECIAL PAGES

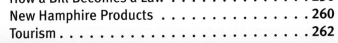

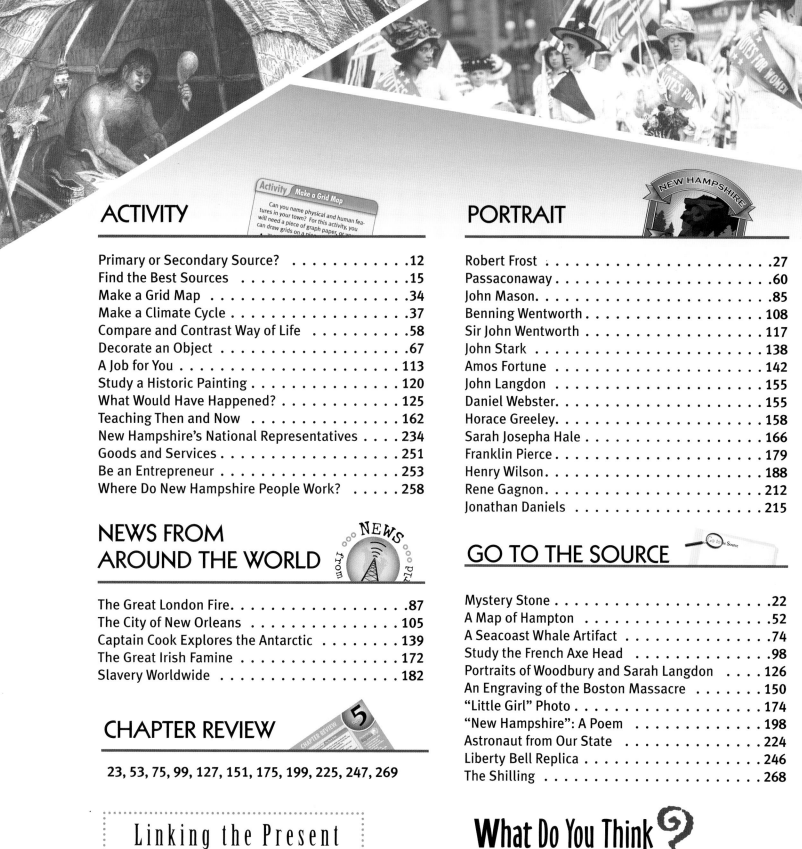

Big Idea

How can we learn about our state?

This is a re-creation of a camp in the 1700s. What clues in the photograph tell you something about New Hampshire's history?

Our New Hampshire Story

The way we live in New Hampshire today is connected to the choices people made in the past. We study our history to learn about the good and bad things that happened long ago so we can make our lives better today.

Key Idea

How will *New Hampshire, Our Home* help us learn about our state?

Words to Understand

caption
century
decade
portrait
timeline

Discovering Your Tools

Welcome to *New Hampshire, Our Home*. Learning about New Hampshire is like going on a great adventure. Have you ever been on one? Maybe you've gone rafting on white-water rapids. You might have tried hiking or rock climbing. What kinds of tools did you need on your adventure? Did you take a flashlight, a life jacket, or ropes? As you study New Hampshire history, you will use some important tools to help you along the way. This textbook is one tool. Let's take a closer look at how this textbook is a tool.

Big Idea

On your adventure through New Hampshire history, you will notice that each chapter begins with a statement called the Big Idea. The Big Idea tells you what the main point of the chapter is.

Opening Picture

On the first page of each chapter, you will also see an opening picture. The picture gives you another clue about the topic the chapter will cover. Someone once said, "A picture is worth a thousand words." What do you think that means?

Introduction Text

Under the chapter number you will see some introduction text that will give you a preview of what you will read about in the chapter. As you read this introduction text, think about what you want to learn from reading the chapter.

Timeline

A timeline is another great tool you will use to understand history. A *timeline* shows on a line when important events happened. By studying a timeline, you can see how historical events fit together.

A timeline can show any amount of time. Sometimes a timeline shows centuries of time. A *century* is 100 years. Sometimes it shows only decades of time. A *decade* is 10 years.

What events would be on a timeline of your life?

Key Idea

Lessons are the next tool you will use on your adventure. Each lesson has a Key Idea. This tells you what the main idea of the lesson is.

Words to Understand

Words to Understand are the words you will need to know to read, write, and talk about information you learned in the lesson. They are highlighted in yellow throughout the chapter.

What Do You Think?

Questions can help you learn new things. As you read, you will come across What Do You Think? questions. These questions ask what *you* think about a social studies topic. There is no right or wrong answer.

Linking the Present to the Past

Have you ever wondered how things that happened long ago affect your life today?

Linking the Present to the Past will help you explore how the past affects your life today. As you read *New Hampshire, Our Home,* you will learn that some things in life change as time goes on, but other things do not.

New Hampshire Portrait

New Hampshire history is filled with stories about interesting people. Reading these stories, which are called New Hampshire Portraits, will help you learn about many people from New Hampshire. A *portrait* is a picture of a person. A New Hampshire Portrait is a word picture of a person's life. Through the portraits, you will learn more about New Hampshire history.

Captions

A *caption* is a description of what a picture shows. Many captions include a question that asks you about something that is shown in the picture.

New Hampshire Inspirations

New Hampshire Inspirations gives you a chance to explore the art and writing of people during each time period in the book. You will learn how men and women used their creative minds to make and write beautiful things.

News from Around the World

Are you ever curious about what is going on in the world? This feature describes events that were happening in other parts of the world at the same time things were happening in New Hampshire. You can see how our state is connected to the rest of our world.

Go to the Source

Go to the Source is an activity that asks you to study an object or a record from the past. This could be a letter, a piece of pottery, or an old picture.

Chapter Review

Once you reach the Chapter Review, you're almost finished! Chapter Review questions and activities help you review and think about what you read in the chapter.

Reviewing the Big Idea questions help you review the information in each lesson.

You Are the Geographer is an activity that helps you build geography skills.

Becoming a Better Reader is an activity that helps you develop reading skills.

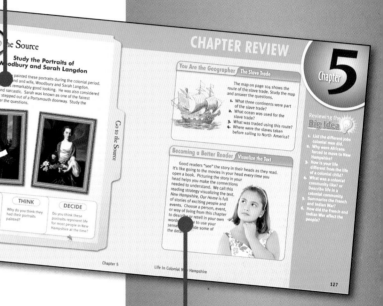

Key Idea Review

Key Idea Review questions are a quick way to help you review what you read in each lesson. Sometimes it is easy to forget. If you do, just go back and read parts of the lesson again.

LESSON ❶ KEY IDEA REVIEW

1. Describe three tools that will help you learn about history.
2. What tools test your knowledge after reading the chapter?
3. What is the purpose of the Big Idea?

Key Idea

How do historians learn about the past?

Words to Understand

artifact
document
evidence
fact
history
opinion
oral history
point of view
primary source
secondary source

What Is History?

In this book you will learn all about our state's history. *History* is the record of the past. It is the story of decisions people made in the past. It is the story of how people lived. Have you heard your grandparents tell stories about their childhood? Do you remember things about your teacher and friends in first grade? All of these things tell something about history.

What Do You Think ?

Did you know you are making history right now? In fact, you make history every day. If someone wrote a book about your life so far, what would some of the chapters be about?

Learning from the Past

In many ways, our lives today are the same as those of people who lived long ago. But our lives are also different in many ways. Studying history helps us understand why some things have stayed the same and why other things have changed.

By studying history, we can understand our state, our country, and our world. We can learn from the past so that we can use the good things from history to make our lives better. We can learn to not repeat the bad things that happened.

Think Like a Historian

People who study history are called historians. As you read *New Hampshire, Our Home,* you can think like a historian, too. To find out what really happened in the past, historians need proof, or ***evidence***. Evidence can come from two types of sources: primary sources and secondary sources.

Things people have in their homes can tell stories about them. What do the things in the photo tell you about the boy? What things in your home tell a story about you?

How can learning about the past affect our decisions today?

Primary Sources

Some evidence comes from people who were at an event when it occurred. This kind of evidence is called a *primary source.*

Photographs

Most photographs are primary sources. They record what happened at a certain moment in time. You can learn a lot by looking at photographs from the past. You can see what people wore, what their homes were like, and how they lived.

You can also learn by comparing photographs of the past to photographs of today. You can see how things have changed. Look at the two photographs below. Can you see how much Manchester has changed over the last 100 years? What do the photos tell you about how transportation has changed? How have the buildings changed?

This is Elm Street in downtown Manchester. The photo was taken in the 1900s. What clues in the photo tell you it was not taken in modern times?

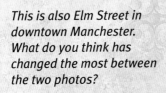

This is also Elm Street in downtown Manchester. What do you think has changed the most between the two photos?

Journals and Letters

Documents, like journals, letters, newspapers, and legal papers, are also primary sources. Journals and diaries can tell us what life was like for early New Hampshire farmers or mill workers. A ship captain's logbook can tell about life at sea. Soldiers' letters can describe life during war.

Oral History

Suppose your grandfather was telling you about his first television set. You could record him as he was talking. You could also write down what he was saying. This is called oral history. *Oral history* is history that people tell out loud. We can learn about the past by listening to stories told by people who lived during other times.

Artifacts

Things people made or used in the past and left behind are called *artifacts.* A Native American basket is an artifact. By looking at the basket, you might learn what materials people had. You might be able to guess how they used those materials. The artifact might lead you to ask new questions. Why did native people need baskets? How did they decide things like the size and shape of the baskets?

Native Americans used baskets for many things. Why do you think this basket is so fancy? What do you think it was used for?

This painting is a secondary source. It shows Concord in the 19th century, but painted after the time period it is showing. What can we learn about Concord using this secondary source?

Secondary Sources

Can you guess what a ***secondary source*** is? It is something written, said, or made by someone who was not there at the time of the event. For example, a modern painting that shows an artist's idea of a past event is a secondary source. This textbook is a secondary source, too!

Secondary sources are important tools to historians. They tell us more about the stories of the past because sometimes they include information that was not known at the time of the event. Good secondary sources are those made or written by historians who have studied primary sources.

Activity | Primary or Secondary Source?

On a piece of paper, number from one to five. For each item below, write a "P" if it is a primary source. Write an "S" if it is a secondary source.

1. A letter written by our first president
2. A modern copy of an old rifle
3. An arrowhead made 6,000 years ago
4. A picture taken during a battle
5. A movie made today about the first airplane flight

Fact vs. Opinion

In history there are facts. A *fact* is something that is true and can be proved. Here are some examples of facts:

- The capital of New Hampshire is Concord.
- There are 12 months in a year.

There are also opinions in history. An **opinion** is something someone thinks or believes. Here are some opinions:

- Strawberry ice cream is better than vanilla.
- I think soccer is fun.

Opinions often have words like *better, best, I think, right,* and *wrong* in them.

It is important to know the difference between facts and opinions. If something is a fact, we can trust that it is true. If something is an opinion, we need to look at some facts or other opinions to get a better idea of the truth.

Point of View

Imagine you and your friend watch a movie together. Afterwards you tell her all the wonderful things you liked about it. You are informing her of your opinion. You are explaining your **point of view.**

Your friend did not enjoy the movie. She tells you all the things she did not like about it. She has a different point of view.

History is filled with stories about people who had different points of view. Sometimes their different ways of looking at things caused changes to happen. For example, when factories were first built in the United States. Some adults wanted older children to work in them. Other adults wanted children to go to school instead. The different points of view caused people to challenge laws and make new ones.

When you study history, it is important to look at many points of view to truly understand what happened.

People have different points of view about everything. For example, some people think our rivers and lakes should be kept beautiful and used only for sports, like fishing. Other people believe we should use our waterways to earn money. They think we should use the water to power mills and move goods, like lumber. How do you think our rivers and lakes should be used?

This wagon can give us information about the past. How do you know it is a primary source?

What do you think this actor at Strawbery Banke could be telling these girls about history?

Using Many Sources

Because there are many points of view, it is important to look at many sources of history. That way we get a more complete picture of what happened. Let's say we look at an artifact, like an old wagon. We might be able to tell how it was made, but how do we know when it was made? How do we know what it carried? Do we know where it went?

We need different sources to answer these questions. We may need maps or diaries. We may need books. Other sources help us get the whole story.

Collecting Pieces of the Past

Sometimes historians do not have enough facts to tell the entire story of a group of people or about an event. Historians collect all the information they can find to help them understand history.

Have you ever visited Strawbery Banke? At this living history museum, actors wear clothing from the past and pretend to be people who lived long ago. The actors study primary sources to learn how people spoke or dressed in the past.

Are you ready to study New Hampshire history? You are going to have many chances to research information about New Hampshire. With so much information out there, be sure to pick the best sources. Go through the following list, and pick which is the best source from each pair. Make sure you can explain your choice.

1. News Web site updated every day **OR** news Web site last updated two days ago
2. History article written by a historian **OR** history article written by a student
3. Newspaper full of opinions **OR** newspaper full of facts
4. Web site that lists its sources **OR** Web site that does not list its sources
5. Magazine full of spelling errors **OR** magazine without spelling errors

LESSON 2 KEY IDEA REVIEW

1. Why do historians study the past?
2. What is the difference between a primary and a secondary source?
3. Why does point of view matter to historians?

Key Idea

What can we learn about New Hampshire from our state symbols and celebrations?

Words to Understand

celebration
emblem
motto
official
represent
seal
symbol

State Symbols and Celebrations

Studying our state symbols and *celebrations* is a fun way to begin learning about New Hampshire's history. A *symbol* is something that stands for something else. All of New Hampshire's state symbols tell us something special about our state.

State Symbols

New Hampshire's state *seal* is a symbol used on government papers to show they are *official*. It shows the sailing ship *Raleigh* with the sun rising behind it. The *Raleigh* was a ship used during the American Revolution. You will read about the Revolution later in this book. Around the *Raleigh* is the phrase "Seal of the State of New Hampshire 1776."

Our state flag is blue with our state seal in the center. The seal is circled by a wreath of laurel leaves with nine stars to represent New Hampshire's place as the ninth state.

Our state *motto* is "Live Free or Die." The words were first written by General John Stark. They were part of a letter General Stark wrote to his soldiers many years after they had fought in a war. What do you think the motto means?

The state *emblem* is used on our state's license plates, highway signs, and quarter. It shows the Old Man of the Mountain, which is a rock formation that used to hang above Profile Lake in the White Mountains. The Old Man of the Mountain was chosen for our state emblem because it *represents* the strength of New Hampshire's people. You will read more about this famous rock formation in the next chapter.

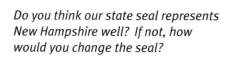

Do you think our state seal represents New Hampshire well? If not, how would you change the seal?

The official state song of New Hampshire is "Old New Hampshire."
Read the words of the first verse and chorus, and imagine the things
they describe about New Hampshire.

"Old New Hampshire"

Written by Dr. John F. Holmes
Composed by Maurice Hoffman Jr.

With a skill that knows no measure,
From the golden store of Fate
God, in His great love and wisdom,
Made the rugged Granite State;
Made the lakes, the fields, the forests;
Made the rivers and the rills;
Made the bubbling, crystal fountains of New Hampshire's Granite Hills.

Chorus:
Old New Hampshire,
Old New Hampshire,
Old New Hampshire, grand and great.
We will sing of Old New Hampshire,
Of the dear old Granite State.

Symbols of New Hampshire

New Hampshire also has many plants, animals, and rocks as state symbols. Let's look at some of them.

State Tree: White Birch

White birch trees were important to Native Americans and early European settlers. They used the strong, bendable bark to make canoes. They also used the bark as writing paper. White birch trees grow throughout our state. They have been called the "Queen of the Woods."

State Wildflower: Pink Lady's Slipper

Pink lady's slipper grows wild. It can be found in moist, wooded areas of our state. It takes a very long time for the plant to grow. Some plants live to be 20 or more years old!

State Flower: Purple Lilac

Purple lilac first traveled from England to America in 1750. It was planted at Governor Benning Wentworth's home in Portsmouth. The plant's purple flowers became popular with early English settlers. Many people began growing them. Today, you can find purple lilac in gardens, on farms, and along roadsides throughout our state.

State Insect: Ladybug

Students in a fifth-grade class helped make the ladybug our state insect after they learned about the insect in social studies. The ladybug is welcome in many gardens because it eats bugs that harm plants. You can also find these insects in grasslands and forests.

State Bird: **Purple Finch**

The small, plump purple finch is our state bird. Its name comes from the feathers on male birds' heads and backs. Females have brown and white feathers. The purple finch lives in our forests and parks. It eats seeds, buds, blossoms, and fruit.

State Animal: **White-Tailed Deer**

White-tailed deer are common in New Hampshire. They eat green leaves, grasses, corn, acorns, nuts, and twigs of woody plants. When they are scared, they raise their tails like a flag. White-tailed deer are very good runners. They can reach speeds close to 30 miles per hour!

State Rock, Gem, and Mineral: **Granite, Smoky Quartz, and Beryl**

Granite is our state rock. It is used to make things like countertops, steps, and roadside curbs. Smoky quartz is our state gem. It is found in granite and other rocks. Beryl is our state mineral. It is also found in granite.

State Fruit: **Pumpkin**

Our newest state symbol is the pumpkin. It was adopted in 2006. The pumpkin grows in all of the state's 10 counties. Many towns celebrate pumpkin festivals every year.

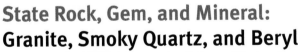

Special Days
of New Hampshire

Holidays are special days that celebrate important events. Some holidays, such as Christmas, Kwanzaa, and Hanukkah, are celebrated by people all over the world. Others are celebrated only in the United States. Two such U.S. holidays are Thanksgiving and Independence Day (the 4th of July).

New Hampshire communities host many celebrations each year. Here are some of them:

Maple Weekend is held in March. Maple sugar producers around our state take visitors on tours of their farms and demonstrate the syrup process.

Every year, people who have moved out of our state return to their New Hampshire hometowns to visit friends and family during Old Home Days.

Each year in June, hundreds of thousands of motorcyclists gather at Weirs Beach in the Lakes Region for Bike Week. They have been coming to the annual gathering from all over the United States and Canada since the early 1900s.

The Colebrook Winter Carnival has ice-carving competitions, snow tube relays, and dogsled rides.

Singers, dancers, magicians, and gymnasts perform at Newport's annual Community Talent Show.

The North Country Moose Festival has been an annual tradition since 1991. It has many crafts for sale, and people gather to eat and enjoy music and shows.

The Keene Pumpkin Festival has been breaking records for the greatest number of lit jack-o'-lanterns in one place at one time since 1991. Nearly 25,000 carved pumpkins line the town's streets each October.

The New Hampshire Highland Games is the largest Scottish cultural festival in the Northeast. For more than 30 years, people have gathered to celebrate the music, dance, customs, and sporting events of their Scottish heritage.

The Hampton Beach Seafood Festival has more than 150,000 visitors each day.

Manchester's annual Made in NH Expo is a great place to view and sample products and services made in our state.

LESSON ③ KEY IDEA REVIEW

1. What is our state motto?
2. Why does each state have symbols?
3. Describe one of New Hampshire's state symbols.

Go to the Source

Mystery Stone

In 1872, construction workers dug up a lump of clay near the shore of Lake Winnipesaukee. This carved stone was within the lump of clay. Archaeologists have wondered where the "Mystery Stone" came from for over 100 years. The Mystery Stone was donated to the New Hampshire Historical Society in 1927. The society does not know of any other findings of a stone like this in the United States.

LOOK	THINK	DECIDE
How would you describe the Mystery Stone?	What do you think the history behind the Mystery Stone could be?	Write three sentences describing what it would have been like to find the Mystery Stone.

Spotlighting Geography / Oral History Report

Geography sometimes influences people to move to different places. Some people prefer warmer climates. Others may enjoy the ocean. Prepare a three- to five-minute oral history report describing why your family came to New Hampshire. Present your oral history report in front of your class.

Reviewing the Big Idea

1. List two things the textbook tools have in common.

2. How is the state emblem used?

3. Write three sentences explaining what a historian does.

4. Compare and contrast the difference between a primary and secondary source.

5. Describe one of the celebrations in New Hampshire and tell why it is important to the people.

6. Create a list of three different sources and tell why they are important.

Becoming a Better Reader / Preview Text Features

In this chapter, you learned that one of the most important reading strategies is hardly reading at all! It's called previewing. You previewed the features of this book and identified the parts of the textbook. Previewing a textbook helps you prepare to read. Preparing to read helps you better understand what you read. After previewing this book, write two sentences about what you might learn by reading *New Hampshire, Our Home*.

Big Idea

How does New Hampshire's geography affect the way people live?

This is a satellite image of Earth. You can see the landmass of North America. Can you find the United States?

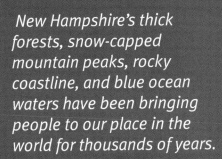

New Hampshire's Place in the World

New Hampshire's thick forests, snow-capped mountain peaks, rocky coastline, and blue ocean waters have been bringing people to our place in the world for thousands of years.

Key Idea

Where in the world is New Hampshire?

Words to Understand

absolute location
cardinal direction
continent
elevation
equator
geography
hemisphere
intermediate direction
latitude
longitude
prime meridian
relative location

The Place We Call Home

Birches

When I see birches bend to left and right
Across the lines of straighter darker trees,
I like to think some boy's been swinging them.
But swinging doesn't bend them down to stay
As ice storms do. Often you must have seen them
Loaded with ice a sunny winter morning
After a rain. They click upon themselves
As the breeze rises, and turn many-colored
As the stir cracks and crazes their enamel.
Soon the sun's warmth makes them shed crystal shells
Shattering and avalanching on the snow crust—

—Robert Frost

The lines above were taken from a poem written by Robert Frost. He lived in New Hampshire for many years. He wrote these words about New Hampshire's state tree, the white birch, to capture the natural beauty of this state. What other things from nature does Robert Frost write about? Do any of them remind you of New Hampshire?

In this chapter you will learn about New Hampshire's geography. **Geography** is the study of Earth's land, water, people, and other living things. Learning about the geography of New Hampshire helps us understand where and how we live. It helps us understand how people, things, and ideas move from one place to another.

Have you ever built a sand castle on Hampton Beach? Have you camped in the White Mountain National Forest? Have you visited mills along the Merrimack River? Have you ever noticed how tree branches, like the ones in Frost's poem, sparkle in the sun after an ice storm? These places and things are part of New Hampshire's geography.

New Hampshire has many white birch trees. You will read more about birch trees later in this book.

ROBERT FROST
1874–1963

Robert Frost was born in San Francisco, California, but lived in New Hampshire for many years. His father died when he was 11 years old. His mother moved the family to Massachusetts, where she worked as a teacher. Robert began writing poetry in high school. He married his high school sweetheart, Elinor. Robert and Elinor became teachers.

The Frosts moved to a farm in Derry and began raising a family. They worked on the farm each day, and Robert wrote poetry at night. No one would publish his poetry at first. He had to go back to work as a teacher to support his family.

After a few years, Robert sold the farm and moved his family to England. Shortly after leaving the United States, his poetry became very popular. The Frosts returned to New Hampshire and bought a house in Franconia.

Robert Frost died in Boston at the age of 88. Today, he is one of our country's most famous poets. Many of his poems are set in New Hampshire's towns and villages. Millions of readers around the world enjoy his descriptions of New Hampshire's countryside.

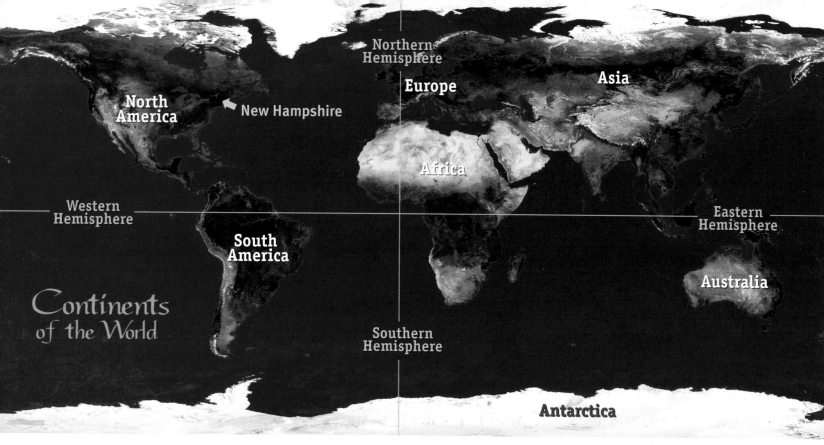

Continents of the World

North America — New Hampshire

Europe

Asia

Africa

Northern Hemisphere

Western Hemisphere

Eastern Hemisphere

South America

Australia

Southern Hemisphere

Antarctica

Where in the World Is New Hampshire?

We live on the planet Earth. But just where on Earth is New Hampshire located? Earth has seven large land areas called **continents.** New Hampshire is on the continent of North America.

North America is divided into three countries. A country is a land area that has its own government. The country we live in is the United States of America. The country south of us is Mexico. Which country is north of us?

The United States is made up of 50 different states. Each state has its own government. Which states are New Hampshire's neighbors?

How Do We Locate a Place?

Imagine your friends who live in a different country want to visit your home. How would you tell them where to find it? There are two ways we can describe a location.

Relative location tells us where a place is in relation to other places or things. For example, New Hampshire is

Planet
▼
Continent
▼
Country
▼
State
▼
County
▼
City or Town
▼
Neighborhood or Farm
▼
Family
▼
Individual

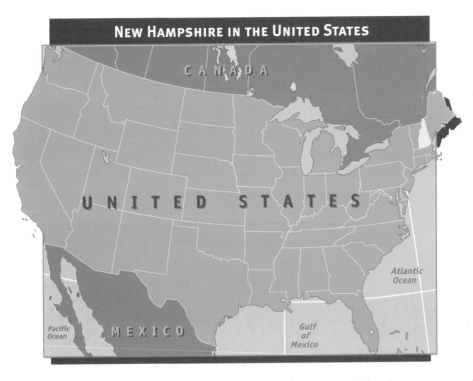

NEW HAMPSHIRE IN THE UNITED STATES

CANADA

UNITED STATES

Atlantic Ocean

Pacific Ocean

MEXICO

Gulf of Mexico

SURROUNDING STATES

CANADA

Maine

Vermont

New Hampshire

Massachusetts

between Maine and Vermont. Your house might be next to the park or five houses away from the school. What is the relative location of your school?

Absolute location is the exact spot where a place can be found. An address is an absolute location. What is the address of your house?

Latitude and Longitude

Look at the globe. Find the *equator*. It is the imaginary line that circles the middle of the globe. It divides Earth into two halves, or *hemispheres*. Imaginary lines that are north and south of the equator are called *latitude* lines.

The imaginary lines running between the North and South poles are called *longitude* lines. They are east and west of the prime meridian. Find the *prime meridian* on the globe. It divides Earth equally into eastern and western hemispheres.

Lines of latitude and longitude cross each other on a globe or map and form a grid.

You can use the grid to find an exact location anywhere on Earth.

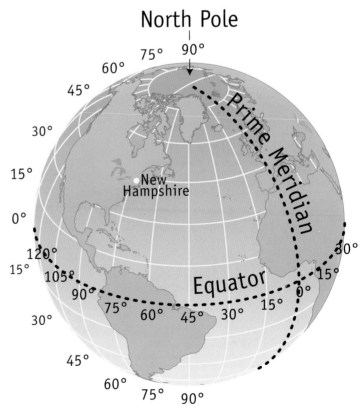

North Pole

New Hampshire

Prime Meridian

Equator

New Hampshire's Place in the World

Reading a Map

Maps help us find our way from one place to another. They help us understand where we are. There are many kinds of maps. There are city maps, maps that show mountains and rivers, and maps that show where important places are. Some maps show the number of people living in a place. Here are some things to look for when you read a map.

TITLE

The first thing to look for on a map is the title. It is usually at the top. It tells what kind of information the map shows.

LEGEND or KEY

Mapmakers use symbols to stand for things like cities, airports, parks, campgrounds, and mountains. A legend, or key, tells what each symbol means. Some maps use colors to show elevation. **Elevation** means how high a place is above the level of the ocean. If you looked at an elevation map of New Hampshire, you would see that the northwestern part of the state is higher in elevation than the southeastern part.

SCALE

To show how far apart things are, mapmakers use a scale. The scale measures the distance between places. One inch on a map might stand for 50 or 100 miles on real land.

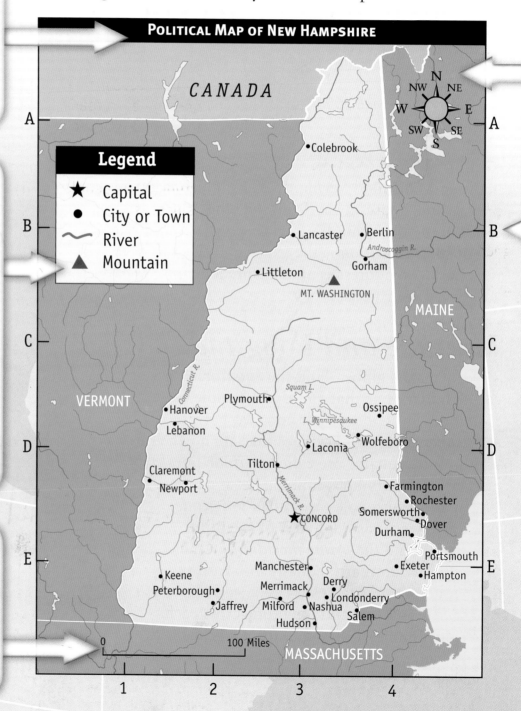

POLITICAL MAP OF NEW HAMPSHIRE

Legend
★ Capital
● City or Town
∿ River
▲ Mountain

COMPASS ROSE

Most maps and globes have a compass rose that shows the four main directions: north, south, east, and west. These directions are called **cardinal directions.** Halfway between north and east is northeast, or NE. This is called an **intermediate direction.** Can you name the other intermediate directions?

MAP GRID

Latitude and longitude lines are one type of map grid. Sometimes maps have grids that use letters and numbers. On the map shown here, numbers run across the bottom of the grid, and letters run along the sides. The location of a place can be described by where it is on the grid.

Using Satellites

In the 1970s, the U.S. military placed 24 satellites 12,000 miles in space above Earth. These satellites send signals back to Earth. On the ground, a global positioning system (GPS) receiver can pick up the signals and find a location based on longitude and latitude. Now people can find locations of homes, businesses, lakes, parks, or anything else. They can simply type in where they want to go, and the GPS will guide them to the locations.

LESSON ① KEY IDEA REVIEW

1. Define geography.
2. What do latitude and longitude lines show?
3. On which continent is New Hampshire located?

Key Idea

What physical features in New Hampshire make it a good place for people to live?

Words to Understand

climate
foliage
glacier
harbor
human feature
humid
notch
physical feature
weather

Farmers built walls like these with rocks that were moved by glaciers. Many of these walls are very old. Have you ever seen one?

Changes Over Time

The geography of a place can change over time. The place we know as New Hampshire did not always look the way it does today. Long ago, winters were very cold and snowy, and they lasted most of the year. Summers did not get warm enough to melt the snow. These long, cold periods are called ice ages. They lasted for thousands of years.

During the ice ages, snow fell in thick layers on the land. The snow deepened into large, slow-moving sheets of ice called *glaciers*. Some of the glaciers were more than a mile thick! Rocks and sand were trapped in the ice as the glaciers got bigger. The rocks and sand gave the glaciers a rough surface, like sandpaper. The glaciers scraped off the tops of mountains and dug deep V-shaped canyons, called *notches,* into Earth.

About 10,000 years ago, the climate in the land that is now New Hampshire began to change. The air warmed, and winters became shorter. Glaciers began to melt into some of the rivers and lakes we see today. Rocks and boulders were left behind, scattered over the land. Have you seen a stone wall in a New Hampshire village or around an old farm pasture? Farmers gathered these stones that were left here by glaciers to create the walls. They used the walls as fences for farm animals and to show their property boundaries.

Crawford Notch was named for members of the Crawford family. They cut a trail to the summit of Mt. Washington.

Dixville

Pinkham

Franconia

Crawford

What Are Notches?

Have you heard of Crawford Notch, Dixville Notch, Franconia Notch, or Pinkham Notch? Why do we call these places "notches"?

Early New Hampshire settlers built their homes out of logs. When cutting down trees, they chopped V-shaped notches in the bases of the trunks. This helped the trees fall away from the woodcutters. The settlers also made V-shaped cuts in the logs to hold their finished cabins together. The narrow passages between the mountains looked like the V shapes in the logs, so the settlers called those places notches, too.

Unique Features

Each place on Earth has features that make it different from other places. Most places have features that make them similar to other places, too. **Physical features** are things made by nature, such as soil, lakes, plants, animals, and climate. **Human features** are things people make, such as cities, homes, bridges, and roads.

When people build human features, they change the physical features of a place. For example, cutting down trees to make room for houses and businesses takes away trees that plants and animals depend on for food and shelter.

It is important to learn about the physical features of our state and to think about ways to protect them when we build human features. Let's look at some of the physical features in New Hampshire.

Activity Make a Grid Map

Can you name physical and human features in your town? For this activity, you will need a piece of graph paper, or you can draw grids on a piece of paper.

1. Think about the physical and human features of your town. Choose five features of your town, such as a school, library, home, river, hill, lake, or hiking trail.

2. Now think about what your town looks like from above, as if you were in an airplane. How is your town spread out?

3. On your grid, draw your town as if you were looking from above. Label each of the five features you chose.

4. Look at your grid map carefully. Which of your five features are physical features? Which are human features?

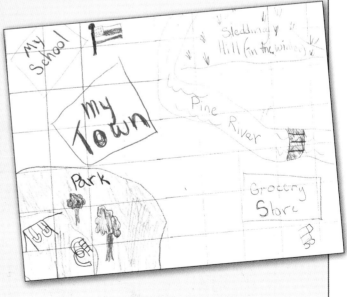

The Atlantic Ocean

The Atlantic Ocean is important for food, transportation, and recreation. People fish in its waters for halibut, cod, and salmon. They also catch lobsters, clams, oysters, and shrimp. Much of the seafood is frozen and sent to places around the United States and the world.

One physical feature of our Atlantic Ocean coastline is Portsmouth Harbor. A *harbor* is a sheltered part of the ocean that is deep enough for ships to sail into. Harbors are protected from strong winds and high waves. The Portsmouth Naval Shipyard is in Portsmouth Harbor. The U.S. Navy repairs submarines there.

The Portsmouth Naval Shipyard is an important human feature in our state. What physical feature surrounds the shipyard?

Spring

Summer

Climate

Climate is another physical feature. **Weather** is how we describe what is going on outside at a certain time. Weather can be sunny or rainy, warm or cold, windy or calm. **Climate** is the weather of a place over a long period of time. Some places have a dry climate, and other places have a rainy climate. Places near the ocean have a different climate from places far from water. One way to learn about the climate of New Hampshire is to describe its four seasons.

In the spring, snow melts into the soil. The ice on rivers and lakes melts. Rainy days and warmer weather cause plants to sprout from the soil. Baby animals are born.

Summers are hot and humid. **Humid** means there is a lot of water in the air that makes your skin feel sticky. Many people go to the beach on summer days. Blueberry and raspberry bushes hang heavy with fruit.

In the fall, the days become cooler. The leaves change colors from deep greens to bright yellows, oranges, and reds. Visitors come from all over the world to see New Hampshire's *foliage*. The warm, sweet smell of hot apple cider drifts through the air at county fairs. Fat pumpkins are stacked high at roadside farm stands.

Winters are cold and wet. The smell of wood smoke swirls from chimneys into the evening air. Snowplows scrape the icy roads in the early morning hours after heavy winter storms. Skiing and hockey are popular sports.

Fall

Winter

The Reasons for the Seasons

Did you know that Earth's movement around the sun causes our seasons? It takes 12 months for Earth to circle around the sun. As Earth circles around the sun, half of it tilts toward the sun, and the other tilts away from the sun. The half that tilts toward the sun gets more light and heat than the half that tilts away. The amount of sun a place gets changes its weather. This means that when it is winter in the Northern Hemisphere, it is summer in the Southern Hemisphere. That is why we have seasons. Each season lasts about three months.

Activity / Make a Climate Cycle

On a blank piece of paper, draw a big circle and divide it into four equal sections. Going clockwise, label each section as one of the four seasons. Make sure you label them in order. For each season, draw what the weather looks like. Then draw one thing you like to do during that season. When you have finished all four seasons, you have drawn the climate of New Hampshire!

The POWER of Weather

Weather can be very powerful in New Hampshire. Sometimes, strong winds blow off the Atlantic Ocean, bringing drenching rains in summer or several feet of snow in winter. These storms are known as "nor'easters."

Two kinds of very serious weather are blizzards and hurricanes. These severe storms are strong and powerful enough to do great damage. Have you experienced one of these extreme storms?

Blizzards

A blizzard is a windstorm that lifts snow off the ground and swirls it through the air. In blizzard conditions, it is hard to see anything around you. The wind piles huge snow drifts against everything in its path. Snow can completely cover cars, road signs, and small buildings.

Hurricanes

Hurricanes form over warm seas and then travel over the ocean. They get stronger as they move. They can grow to be as many as 500 miles across and have wind gusts of up to 225 miles per hour (mph)! When a hurricane gets close to land, its violent winds and rains can rip trees out of the ground and flatten buildings. A hurricane creates enormous ocean waves that crash on the land, destroying homes and businesses in its path.

Blizzards like this can be very dangerous. They can cause traffic accidents, blow over power lines, and bury cars. Have you ever been in a blizzard like this?

LESSON ② KEY IDEA REVIEW

1. Name two physical features and two human features of New Hampshire.
2. What causes the seasons?
3. What physical features can cause the winter to be dangerous?

Regions of the United States

West

Washington
Oregon
Idaho
Nevada
California
Alaska
Hawaii

Montana
Wyoming
Utah
Colorado
Arizona
New Mexico

Midwest

North Dakota
South Dakota
Nebraska
Kansas
Oklahoma
Texas

Minnesota
Wisconsin
Iowa
Missouri

Michigan
Illinois
Indiana
Ohio

Northeast

New Hampshire
Vermont
New York
Pennsylvania

Maine
Massachusetts
Rhode Island
Connecticut
New Jersey
Delaware
Maryland
West Virginia
Virginia

Kentucky
Tennessee
Arkansas
Mississippi
Louisiana
Alabama
Georgia
South Carolina
North Carolina
Florida

Southwest

Southeast

Key Idea

Why is New Hampshire divided into regions?

Words to Understand

lowland
marsh
quarry
region
seaport
upland

What Are Regions?

The world is very big, so one way we can learn about it is to think of it in smaller parts. We call these parts regions. A *region* is an area of land that shares common features. Some regions have mountains. Others have deserts. Some regions are near oceans. Others have big cities. You can live in many different regions at the same time.

We can divide the United States into regions using geography. Many parts of the country have similar climates and are home to the same plants and animals. For example, in the Southwest region the land is very dry. There are many deserts. Cacti, sagebrush, snakes, and jackrabbits live there. Look at the map of the United States above. What five main regions are shown?

Northeast

Southeast

Midwest

Southwest

West

A Place Called New England

New Hampshire is also located in a region called New England. New England is a small region inside the bigger region of the Northeast. It is made up of six states: Maine, Massachusetts, Connecticut, Rhode Island, Vermont, and New Hampshire.

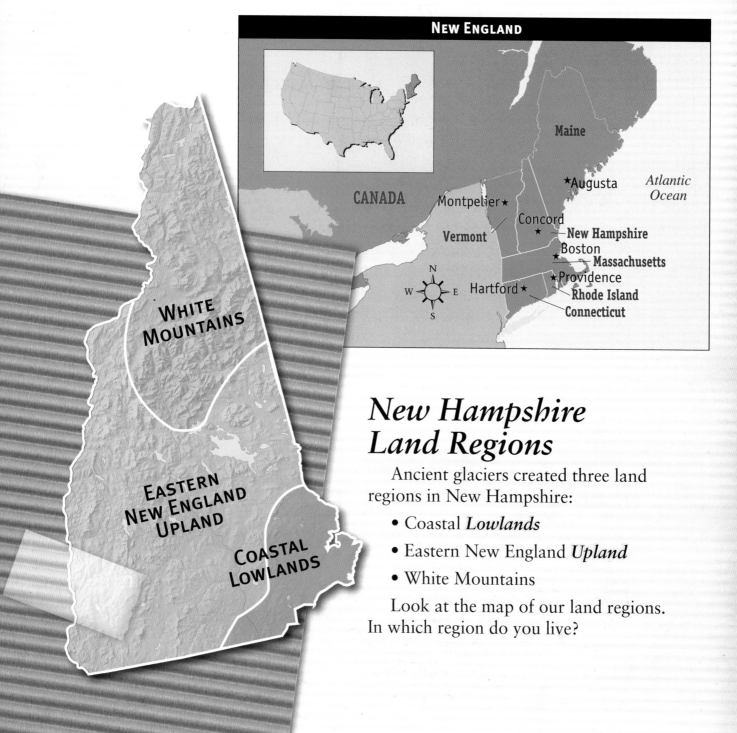

NEW ENGLAND

Maine

Atlantic Ocean

★Augusta

CANADA

Montpelier ★

Concord ★

New Hampshire

Vermont

Boston ★

Massachusetts

★Providence

Hartford ★

Rhode Island

Connecticut

N
W E
S

WHITE MOUNTAINS

EASTERN NEW ENGLAND UPLAND

COASTAL LOWLANDS

New Hampshire Land Regions

Ancient glaciers created three land regions in New Hampshire:

- Coastal *Lowlands*
- Eastern New England *Upland*
- White Mountains

Look at the map of our land regions. In which region do you live?

Coastal Lowlands

Sandy beaches, salt *marshes,* and flat land are some of the physical features in the Coastal Lowlands. Cities, small towns, docks, and bridges are some of its human features. Portsmouth is a big city in this region. It is our state's only seaport. A *seaport* is a city or town by the ocean where ships load and unload cargo.

There are nine islands offshore called the Isles of Shoals. Four of these islands are part of New Hampshire. The rest belong to Maine.

People who live in the Coastal Lowlands have many different kinds of jobs. Some catch fish or lobsters each day to sell to restaurants and stores. Other people work in hotels or museums, helping visitors enjoy the physical and human features of our state. Many people work or attend school at the University of New Hampshire in Durham.

Farmington
Somersworth Rochester
Dover
Durham Portsmouth
Exeter Rye
Derry Hampton
Merrimack
Salem

Portsmouth is one of the biggest cities in New Hampshire. What physical and human features do you see here?

New Hampshire has the shortest shoreline (18.5 miles) of any coastal state. Most of it is open for public use. What do you like to do at the beach?

Eastern New England Upland

What Do You Think?

People live, work, and play in all areas of our state. But most people live in the Eastern New England Upland region. Why do you think the southern part of our state is home to the greatest number of people?

Swenson Granite Works

The Eastern New England Upland region covers more than half our state. It has hills, river valleys, and hundreds of lakes. The Merrimack Valley, the Lakes Region, and the Connecticut River Valley are part of the Eastern New England Upland.

Throughout the state's history, the Merrimack Valley has been a location for many businesses. In the past, water from the Merrimack River was used to power machines in large factories. Today, the region is home to computer companies and banking offices. Many years ago, granite quarries were also common in this region. A *quarry* is a place where rock is taken out of the ground. Today, Swenson Granite Works is one of the few quarries still at work. It is located just outside Concord.

The Lakes Region contains most of our state's major lakes, like Lake Winnipesaukee and Squam Lake. The Connecticut River Valley surrounds the longest river in New England. Water from the Connecticut River provides rich soil for farmers. Mount Monadnock in the southwestern section is one of the best-known physical features of the Eastern New England Upland region.

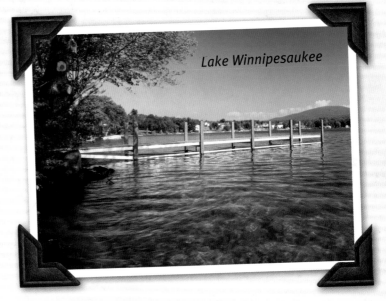

Lake Winnipesaukee

White Mountains

The White Mountains region covers the northern part of our state. It has high mountains, narrow valleys, waterfalls, and streams. Its peaks are covered with snow throughout much of the year. Mount Washington, the highest point in New England (6,288 feet), is located there.

The White Mountains region includes a section called the North Country. Rivers and forests are important physical features in the North Country. The town of Berlin is one of its few human features.

Many people in the White Mountains region work at ski resorts, state parks, and hotels. Others work as loggers, cutting down trees. Some people work in factories or sawmills that make trees into paper, furniture, or lumber for houses.

What Do You Think?

Why do you think there are few human features in the North Country? Do you think this could change in the future? If so, what might cause this to change?

Colebrook

Berlin

Whitefield • Gorham
Littleton
Mt. Washington

Conway •

Mount Washington (above) is the most well-known physical feature in the White Mountains region. Mount Washington Resort is a fancy hotel in the White Mountains. It is over 100 years old! Have you ever visited the resort? Does it look like a nice place to stay?

The Mountains of New Hampshire

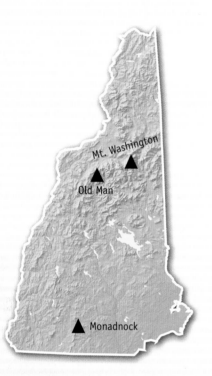

New Hampshire's highest and most famous mountain, Mount Washington, is in the White Mountains region.

It was named for George Washington, the first U.S. president. It is part of a mountain range called the Presidential Range, where most of the peaks are named after presidents.

The climate at the top of Mount Washington is different from the climate in any other part of our state. The mountain is home to some of the worst weather in the world. Scientists work in an observatory located at the mountain's top. An observatory is a building with special instruments that allow scientists to study the weather. In 1934, scientists recorded the world's fastest wind speed—231 mph—blowing across the peak of Mount Washington.

Cold temperatures, strong winds, fog, snow, and ice limit the types of plants and animals that can live near the top of Mount Washington. Only a few tiny plants and trees have been able to adapt to the mountain's harsh conditions.

The Mount Washington Observatory stays frozen most of the year. How do you think scientists get to the observatory in the winter?

Another famous New Hampshire mountain is located in the Eastern New England Upland region between Jaffrey and Keene. It is called Mount Monadnock. Monadnock is a Native American word that means "a mountain that stands alone." Hiking to the top of Mount Monadnock became a popular pastime in the 19th century. Today, it is one of the most frequently climbed mountains in the world. If you hike to the peak on a clear day, you can see all the way to Boston!

Mount Monadnock

Old Man of the Mountain

The Old Man of the Mountain was a series of five granite ledges above Profile Lake in the White Mountains. Viewed from far away, the stone structure looked like the jagged side of a face.

Created by glaciers more than 10,000 years ago, the rock formation was discovered by settlers around 1805. The Old Man inspired author Nathaniel Hawthorne to write a short story called *The Great Stone Face*.

For nearly 200 years, the Old Man of the Mountain symbolized the strength of New Hampshire's people.

In May 2003, after surviving thousands of years of wind, snow, and rain, the famous formation fell. If you visit the area today, you can look through special viewfinders near the base of the cliff to see how the Old Man used to look.

LESSON ③ KEY IDEA REVIEW

1. What are the three regions in New Hampshire?
2. Why does each region have different physical features?
3. In which U.S. region is New Hampshire? In which New Hampshire region is your town?

Key Idea

What natural resources in New Hampshire do people use?

Words to Understand

bog
ecosystem
natural resource
nonrenewable
preserve
renewable
wetland

Trees are a very important natural resource for our state. What is this tractor moving? What kinds of things can we do with trees?

Using Our Land

Natural resources are things found in nature that people use. The ways we use our natural resources determine how we live and often where we live in our state. Two of New Hampshire's natural resources are soil and water.

What Grows in Our Soil?

New Hampshire is a small state, but it is home to many different kinds of plants that depend on its soil.

Trees

Most of New Hampshire's land is covered with trees. They provide clean air, homes for animals, and scenic areas for everyone to enjoy.

Trees also provide wood, which people use to make paper, furniture, cabinets, baskets, and lumber. Many of New Hampshire's trees are cut down each day and loaded onto big trucks. The trucks take the logs to mills, where they are cut into lumber for construction or ground into pulp for paper.

Many people depend on New Hampshire's forests for jobs and natural resources. But many animals also depend on forests for shelter and food.

People have taken three important steps to help protect New Hampshire's forests.

- They have made careful plans about which trees to cut and how best to use them.
- They have planted seeds for new trees to replace many of those that have been cut down.
- They have set aside sections of land where logging is not allowed.

Crops

New Hampshire farms produce many different crops, especially in the Connecticut River Valley. Apples, Christmas trees, strawberries, blueberries, and vegetables are among the many products farmers grow in our state. Farmers also raise cows for milk, bees for honey, and maple trees for maple syrup. Many towns have market days, where people can buy right from local farmers.

What's So Special About Maple Trees?

One of our state's most popular trees is the sugar maple. Maples grow well in New Hampshire's cold climate and rocky soil.

In fall, maple leaves turn from green to shades of yellow, orange, and red. Each spring, farmers use sap from maple trees to make syrup. It takes about 40 gallons of sap to make one gallon of syrup.

Have you had maple syrup on pancakes? What other foods do you eat with maple syrup?

At a farmers' market you can buy fresh fruits and vegetables from local farmers. Why do you think there are so many strawberries and blueberries at this market?

How Do We Use Water?

We use water for food, sports, businesses, transportation, and many other things. Let's look at the water sources in our state.

Lakes and Rivers

Our state has more than 1,300 lakes and ponds and about 40 rivers. Swimming, sailing, boating, windsurfing, canoeing, kayaking, and fishing are popular water sports in our state's sparkling blue lakes. Ice fishing and ice skating are fun when lakes and ponds freeze in winter.

Businesses also use our many waterways. Before there were refrigerators, workers at the Fresh Pond Ice Company in Brookline chopped ice from frozen lakes. They sold the blocks to homes and stores in New Hampshire and Massachusetts. The Amoskeag Manufacturing Company used the Merrimack River to operate huge mills.

Most of New Hampshire's towns and cities are located near a river. Can you think of other reasons why rivers are so important in our state?

Brookline

Fly-fishing is a popular sport in our state. What other sport is shown in this photo?

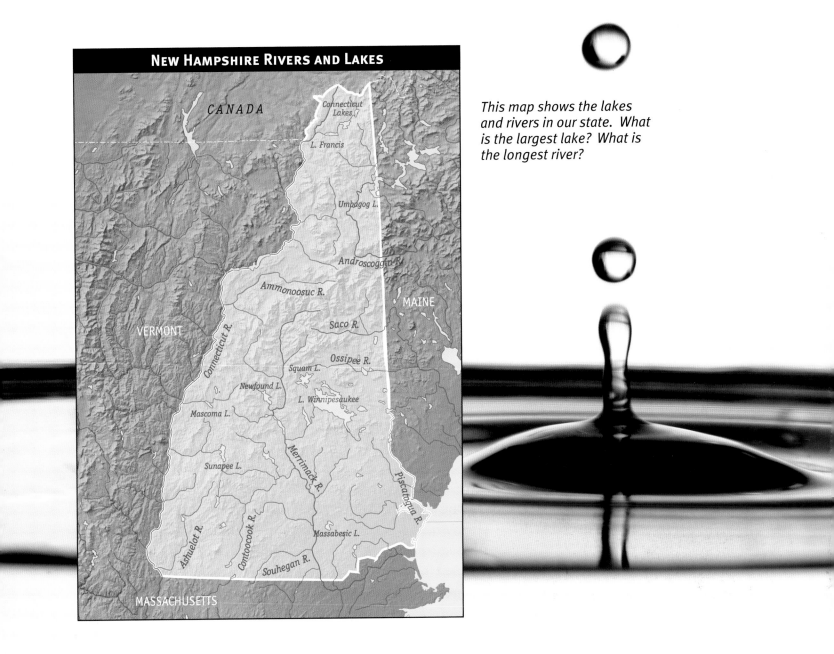

NEW HAMPSHIRE RIVERS AND LAKES

This map shows the lakes and rivers in our state. What is the largest lake? What is the longest river?

Wetlands

Another type of water in New Hampshire is called a wetland. A **wetland** is a low area of land that is covered by water long enough for plants to grow. It is a type of ecosystem. An **ecosystem** is a community of plants and animals that depend on each other to live. Salt marshes and swamps are two types of wetlands. Salt marshes are wet areas near the ocean where fresh and salt water mix.

A **bog** is a wet area of land with trees or shrubs. If you walk near a bog, you will notice that the air feels heavy. It smells like wet soil and mossy plants.

There are many plants and animals that live in this wetland. What kinds of animals do you think live here?

As more people and businesses move into New Hampshire, wetlands are in danger of being destroyed. Many town and city governments have made laws about how close to wetlands people can build homes and roads. Why do you think it is important for us to protect our wetlands?

Renewable and Nonrenewable Resources

Some of our resources are **renewable**. That means they will always come back. For example, if you cut down a tree, you can plant another one. We use wood from trees to build homes and make paper. By planting new trees, we make sure we always have wood.

Other resources are **nonrenewable**. When those resources are used up, they are gone forever. We depend on nonrenewable resources like oil to make gasoline to fuel our cars, buses, and airplanes. As we use up the Earth's supply of oil, we will need new ways to power our cars.

Granite is a type of hard rock. It is another nonrenewable resource. Many of the stones and boulders you see scattered across our countryside are granite.

Granite's strength and beauty have made it popular for constructing buildings. New Hampshire granite has been used for buildings all over the United States. Today, there are only a few working granite quarries in our state.

Preserving Our Resources

From the time people first came to New Hampshire, they changed the land. They hunted animals and cleared forests. They chopped down the trees to build homes and make paper. They built businesses and factories on rivers and wetlands.

Many people believe more should be done to protect our land and resources. Others believe the land should be used for homes and businesses. Still others say we must find a balance between changing the land to support ourselves and *preserving* the land from any change.

When you turn 18 years old, you will be able to vote. You will join other adults in making decisions for the good of all the people in the state. By studying the history and geography of New Hampshire, you will have a better understanding of the past. You will be able to help your state make better decisions for the future.

How are these kids preserving natural resources?

LESSON ④ KEY IDEA REVIEW 🔑

1. Why are trees so important?
2. Name two types of water ecosystems.
3. What is the difference between renewable and nonrenewable resources?

Go to the Source

A Map of Hampton

Maps help us find our way from one place to another. They help us understand where we are. The map below has been re-created from maps and ancient records in 1892. It shows homes of the original settlers of Hampton. Study the map and answer the questions.

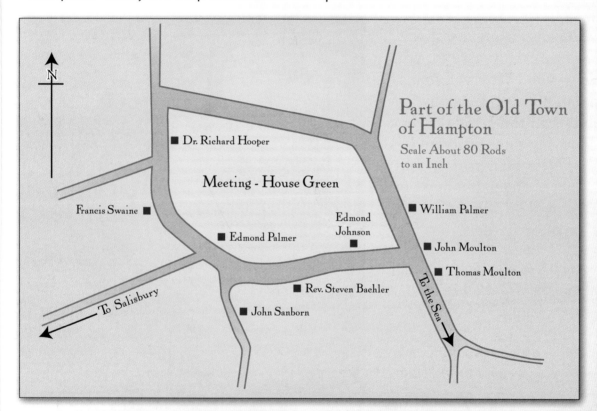

LOOK

What parts of the map stand out to you the most?

THINK

How might these roads have changed since then?

DECIDE

Do you think these roads are still in use today? Write three sentences explaining your opinion.

CHAPTER REVIEW

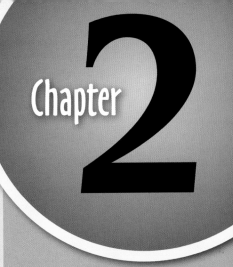

Spotlighting Geography / Reading a Road Map

Roads are human features. The blacktop, the material used to make roads, comes from oil. Oil is a natural resource. Roads help people and goods move from place to place.

Have an adult help you find a road map. Practice reading a road map by answering the following questions:

1. What is the title of the map?
2. What symbols does the map use to show features?
3. What is the scale of miles on the map?
4. Where is the compass rose located on the map?
5. What could you use the map for?
6. What area does the map cover?

Becoming a Better Reader / Reading for Information

This lesson provided a lot of information about the geography of New Hampshire. To understand the information in this chapter, we learned to read a map, organize information, and look for relationships. As you continue reading about the history of New Hampshire, think about these three ways to understand new information. Draw a picture to show some of the information you learned from this chapter.

Reviewing the Big Idea

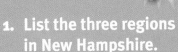

1. List the three regions in New Hampshire.
2. Explain the importance of protecting our environment.
3. How can you apply your map skills to everyday life?
4. Compare and contrast the difference between a physical and human feature.
5. Assess the ways we use our renewable and nonrenewable resources. Are we doing a good job? If not, how can we do better?
6. Create directions from your house to school in five simple steps.

Big Idea

Who were the first people to live in what is now New Hampshire, and how did they live before the Europeans came to America?

These Native Americans are hunting moose. The people did much more with the moose besides eat its meat. Can you think of other ways Native Americans might have used the moose?

Timeline of Events

9000 B.C. – 7000 B.C.
Paleo-Indian Period

9000 B.C.   6000 B.C.   3000 B.C.

7000 B.C.– 1000 B.C.
Archaic Period

8000 B.C.
• Humans arrive in the area now called New Hampshire.
• The last ice age ends.

Native Americans

The story of our state began long before European explorers mapped its coastline. For thousands of years, the rivers, lakes, mountains, and valleys we know as New Hampshire were home to Native American families.

A.D. 1620
Passaconaway becomes the leader of the Pennacook tribe.

1000 B.C. – A.D. 1600
Woodland Period

| A.D. 0 | A.D. 500 | A.D. 1000 | A.D. 1500 |

1000S
The Abenaki arrive in the region now known as New Hampshire.

1500S
First documented encounters between Native Americans and European explorers in New Hampshire

55

Key Idea

Who were the first people to live in what is now New Hampshire, and how did they live?

Words to Understand

adapt
ancestor
archaeologist
culture
descendant
migrate
nomad
prehistoric
sachem
tribe

During the last ice age, the low level of the oceans exposed an area of land that connected today's Asia and North America. How might history have been different if this land bridge never existed?

Ten Thousand Winters Ago

The last ice age ended about 10,000 years ago. Plants began to grow in soil once covered by glaciers. Large animals roamed thick forests. Finally, the first people arrived in the place we call New Hampshire.

The first people to live here were **descendants** of people who **migrated**, or moved, to North America long ago. Historians believe many of the first humans on our continent migrated from Asia across a land bridge over the Bering Strait. They were **nomads** who traveled from place to place, hunting animals for food.

Humans did not travel to North America in one large group. They did not follow maps or plan how far they would go before they stopped. Instead, people came in many groups over thousands of years.

Today we call the people who lived here thousands of years ago Native Americans. Native means they were the first people to live here. We also call them Indians.

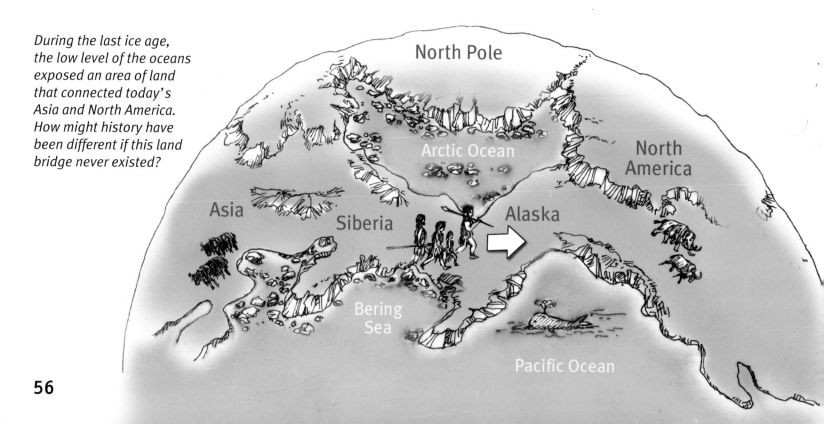

North Pole

Arctic Ocean

North America

Asia

Siberia

Alaska

Bering Sea

Pacific Ocean

Prehistoric People

Early New Hampshire people lived in what we call *prehistoric* times. This means they lived before written records were made. *Archaeologists* group prehistoric people into three different time periods. Each period lasted thousands of years. Changes in climate and the land happened very slowly over time. These changes caused people to *adapt* their ways of doing things in order to survive.

To learn about prehistoric people, modern archaeologists study artifacts early people left behind.

Since we have no written records about prehistoric people, archaeologists study artifacts from those times. They study rock art, fire pits, animal bones, and many other things. Is this drawing a primary or secondary source?

Prehistoric spearheads, knives, and pottery have been found in Manchester. These artifacts give clues about how prehistoric people lived and worked.

Prehistoric Time Periods

Paleo-Indian Period

Time: 11,000 to 9,000 years ago

Climate: Cold and wet, glaciers melted and retreated

Way of Life: Nomadic hunters

Food Sources: Hunted large beasts such as mammoths and saber-toothed tigers

Tools: Stone tools such as spearheads called Clovis points

Archaic Period

Time: 9,000 to 3,000 years ago

Climate: Gradually warmed

Way of Life: People became more settled and traveled less in search of food

Food Sources: Gathered plants and hunted smaller animals such as moose, deer, and fish

Tools: Spearheads, scrapers, knives, and hammers

Woodland Period

Time: 3,000 to 400 years ago

Climate: Continued to warm

Way of Life: People created permanent villages

Food Sources: Hunted, fished, and planted fruits and vegetables

Tools: Pottery made from clay, stones, shells, and plant fibers

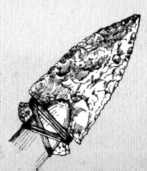

Activity — Compare and Contrast Way of Life

Use the chart to answer the questions.

1. How did the way of life change from one period to the next?
2. Identify two reasons why the way of life changed.
3. How do you think improvements in tools changed life for Native Americans?
4. Compare the climates of the Paleo-Indian and Woodland periods.
5. Look at the food sources. Draw a picture of how the food sources changed from one period to the next. How is this different from our food sources today?

Historic Native Americans

About 400 years ago, European explorers sailed along the Atlantic Coast of New England. They were the first to keep written records about what is now New Hampshire.

As the Europeans explored the land, they met a group of Indians called the Abenaki. The explorers wrote about the native people in their journals. Because we have written records of the Abenaki, they are called historic Native Americans.

The Abenaki

Archaeologists have found tools and pottery that show the Abenaki people lived in the northern part of New England about 1,000 years ago. Many archaeologists believe the Abenaki are descendants of prehistoric people who migrated to North America.

But many Abenaki people today do not believe their *ancestors* came from other places. Instead, they believe a powerful spirit named Gluskonba created their ancestors in North America. Both points of view are important in learning about the early Abenaki people.

Unlike prehistoric Indians, the Abenaki had permanent year-round settlements. They grew crops, so they did not have to depend as much on hunting and gathering food to survive. The Abenaki were divided into separate *tribes,* or groups.

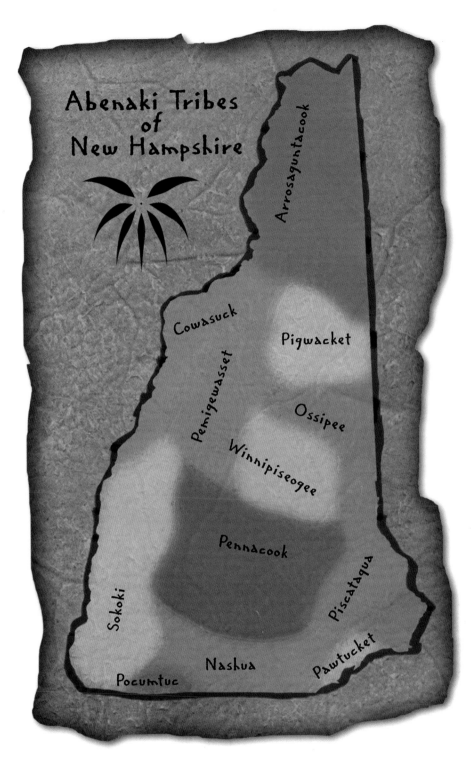

This map shows the different Abenaki tribes that live in today's New Hampshire. Have you ever heard any of these names?

PASSACONAWAY
c. 1555–c. 1670

Passaconaway was the leader of the Abenaki Pennacook tribe. Before the arrival of Europeans, Abenaki tribes formed the Pennacook Confederation. The confederation was a group of tribes that worked together on common problems and joined together for celebrations. Passaconaway led the confederation. One of his most important duties was to unite the Abenaki tribes to protect their villages from enemies like the Mohawk Indians.

When Europeans began building homes and towns on Abenaki lands, Passaconaway tried to keep peace.

Passaconaway lived near Amoskeag Falls in what is now Manchester. He was brave in war and generous to his people. It is believed he lived to be more than 115 years old.

According to Abenaki legend, when Passaconaway died, his body was placed on a sled and pulled by wolves to the top of Mount Washington. There, he disappeared into a cloud of fire and vanished into the sky. No one knows for sure when and where Passaconaway died.

A Common Culture

Native Americans in New England shared a similar *culture,* or way a group of people lives. Their languages, homes, clothes, and spiritual beliefs had many common features.

But Native Americans were not simply a large group of people who did everything the same. They did not share the same family backgrounds. They did not all know each other. They did not follow rules given by a single leader.

Each Abenaki community had its own *sachem,* or leader. A sachem guided his people in making decisions. He could not make people do things they did not want to do. The Abenaki believed people were responsible for making their own decisions.

LESSON ① KEY IDEA REVIEW 🗝

1. What does *prehistoric* mean?
2. Why do archaeologists use artifacts?
3. Which group did the Europeans meet while exploring?

People of the Dawnland

The Abenaki watched the sun rise each morning in the east. They believed it shone down on them before all other people. *Abenaki* means "people of the dawnland." The people respected Earth and all living things. They believed the sky, water, soil, and trees were all gifts from the spirit world to the people. Everything on Earth was part of a great web of life. The Abenaki saw themselves as part of that web. They protected and cared for the land.

Villages

The Abenaki lived in small villages near rivers, lakes, and forests. A village could be home to a few hundred people and could have anywhere from 5 to 50 buildings. Sometimes the people built a high, wooden wall around an entire village to protect it. Why do you think the people chose to live in small villages?

Key Idea

How did the Abenaki live?

Words to Understand

breechcloth
longhouse
moccasin
sapling
sinew
weir
wigwam

What Do You Think

Why do you think water and wood were important to the location of an Abenaki village?

Everyone worked hard in an Abenaki village to keep it running. What jobs do you see being done here?

Notice all of the natural resources being used in this picture. How long do you think it took to build this longhouse?

A family usually had several dogs. Men trained them to help hunt and to bark if a stranger approached the village. The dogs slept inside the longhouses and wigwams.

Wigwams were much smaller than longhouses. How does this wigwam look different from the longhouse? How does it look the same?

Homes

Families lived in two different types of houses. A *longhouse* was shared by many families, especially during winter months. Families also lived in *wigwams*. Usually, one or two families shared a wigwam.

Longhouses

To build a longhouse, the men wedged long, flexible *saplings,* or young trees, into the ground to form an oval shape. Then they bent and tied the saplings together. Women laid bark strips or deerskins over the entire house to keep out wind, rain, and snow. Holes were made in the roof so smoke from fires could escape.

Families slept along the walls in bunks made of woven grass. They used deerskin or bear fur blankets.

Wigwams

Longhouses were not easy to take down and rebuild, so during hunting months, families lived in wigwams. Wigwams were easy to build, take apart, and carry to new locations.

To build a wigwam, the Abenaki put saplings into the ground in a circle. Then they tied the saplings into a dome shape. Women covered the wigwam with mats made from leaves or bark strips. They also covered the entrances with mats, deerskin, or bark. The inside of the wigwam looked a lot like a longhouse.

Working Together

Everyone in an Abenaki community had work to do each day. The people did not record the work they did. Historians use primary sources to interpret what kinds of jobs families did long ago.

Men's Work

If you were a young boy in an Abenaki family, your father would have taught you how to protect your family and provide food.

Hunting and Fishing

Hunting was the main source of food during winter and spring months. Men and boys hunted moose, bear, and deer for food and fur. They used bows, arrows, and knives to kill prey. They used special traps to catch otters and beavers.

Fishing was another important source of food. In spring and fall, men and boys caught fish in rivers and lakes.

Men had several ways to catch fish. They used branches or stones to build fences called *weirs* across streams. The weirs trapped the fish and then fishermen speared or captured them with nets. Nets were also used to catch fish as they swam over small waterfalls.

Building Canoes

Men built canoes to travel on rivers and lakes. They made them by bending strips of wood into a frame and then sewing birch bark to the outside. The birch bark canoe was easy to handle. It could carry heavy loads and move quickly through water.

Men also made canoes by digging out the trunk of a white pine tree. They hollowed out the trunk by burning and scraping its insides. The dugout canoe was strong and dependable, but it was very heavy. It was used on large lakes and for ocean travel.

Abenaki boys spent much of their day learning from their fathers and other men. What are the boys learning to do here?

Abenaki people believed they should respect animals or the animals would no longer allow themselves to be caught. One way the Abenaki showed respect was to carefully bury animal bones they were not able to use. They performed a small ceremony to thank the animal for giving up its life.

Bark from birch trees was flexible and waterproof. Why would this be good for making canoes?

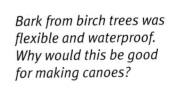

The Abenaki did not have cars, bicycles, or horses. To travel over water, they used canoes.

To travel over land, they walked over miles of trails that connected Native American villages. The trails were narrow, so people often walked in single lines.

In the winter, the people used snowshoes. The frames were made of wood and strips of leather. The special shoes helped people walk on top of the snow instead of sinking into it.

Snowshoes keep you from sinking into the snow by spreading your weight over a wider area. Have you ever worn snowshoes?

Women's Work

If you were a young girl in an Abenaki family, you and your mother would have worked very hard each day to provide food and clothing for your family's needs.

Preparing Food

Abenaki women and girls gathered nuts, fruits, and berries. They picked wild plants for food and medicine. They tapped maple trees for sap and boiled it into syrup. Women also planted corn, beans, and squash. These vegetables were called "the three sisters" because they were planted together. Bean vines climbed up the cornstalks, and squash provided a ground cover that helped hold water in the soil.

Women preserved meat and fish for the winter. They spread out the meat and fish on a wooden rack above a fire. The heat dried the meat and kept it from spoiling or rotting. Women preserved vegetables and fruits by slicing them, removing their seeds, and drying them in open air.

Women dried fish over fires like this one. What do you think the air smelled like while the fish were drying?

Linking the Present to the Past

Today, most people get food at grocery stores and restaurants. People buy clothes and tools at department stores. Native Americans depended on nature to meet their needs. How did they use nature to meet their needs?

Mortars and Pestles

Mortars were made out of stone or wood. They had a dent in the center. A woman used a stone pestle to grind corn, nuts, berries, or herbs in the mortar.

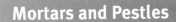

Linking the Present to the Past

Do you eat corn, beans, corn bread, corn chowder, or squash? The Abenaki ate those foods, too. An Abenaki child from long ago would recognize many of the foods your family eats today.

Women knew it was time to plant corn when the spring leaves on oak trees grew to the size of squirrels' ears. Is this woman planting, tending, or harvesting the corn?

Corn and Beans

Corn and beans were two of the most important foods for Native Americans. Women cooked corn and added it to other vegetables, fruits, nuts, and fish. Corn was ground into flour and baked into bread or cake. People ate beans and cooked them into bread. Corn and beans could be dried and saved for the winter months.

An Abenaki mother carried her baby with her wherever she went. The baby was placed into a cradle board and rode on his mother's back as she gathered food, made clothes, and cooked.

Making Clothing

Women and girls made all the clothing for their families. They used animal skins for fabric, tiny animal bones for needles, and long animal *sinews,* or tendons, as thread.

In the summer, boys and girls wore a belt and breechcloth. A *breechcloth* was a piece of animal skin tied around the hips and thighs. Girls covered their breechcloth with a skirt and a long shirt. In the winter, boys and girls wore robes made from beaver fur or moose hide.

Everyone wore *moccasins* throughout the year. The moccasins were usually made from moose fur and leather. In the winter, the Abenaki added a layer of rabbit fur or other animal skin to the outside of the shoes.

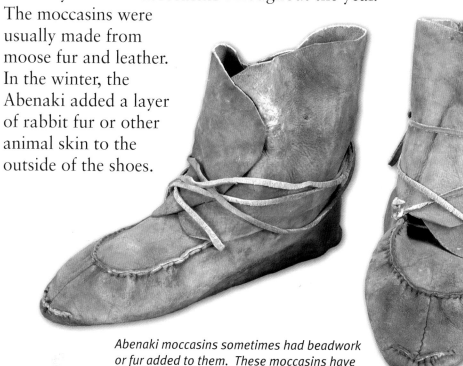

Abenaki moccasins sometimes had beadwork or fur added to them. These moccasins have leather ties that wrap around the ankles. Why would this be useful?

THE CREATIVE ABENAKI

The Abenaki were creative people. They used art to decorate many of the things they used each day. For example, men carved patterns into canoes, and women wove colors into baskets like the one on the left. But using special colored patterns did not make tools stronger or more dependable. Why do you think people took time to add beautiful features to ordinary things?

Activity **Decorate an Object**

Think of an object you use every day at school or at home. Choose something like a pencil, a toothbrush, or a backpack. Make a drawing of the object. Think of a way to decorate it to make it more fun to use or more enjoyable to look at. For example, you could color the object, glue fabric or buttons onto it, or tie ribbons onto it. After you have finished decorating your picture, ask a parent or your teacher for permission to decorate the real object.

LESSON 2 KEY IDEA REVIEW

1. What were Abenaki homes called?
2. Name one thing men and women did daily.
3. What kind of shoes did the Abenaki wear?

Key Idea

What were some of the cultural connections of the Abenaki, and how do they relate to our cultural way of life?

Words to Understand

ceremony
fast
legend
moral
shaman
social
tradition
vision quest

Spiritual Connections

It is said among my people that we were created by Ktsi Nwaskw from the ash tree. At that time long ago, Ktsi Nwaskw gave us permission to use Aki, the Earth, and its bounty with care and respect. We renew that permission by ceremony and prayer to assure harmony and balance of the world.

—*Frederick M. Wiseman, Abenaki tribal member, 2006*

The Abenaki believed the sun, moon, wind, and rain each had special powers. They did special dances to give thanks for good fortune received from nature.

Shamans

The Abenaki looked to shamans for guidance and protection. They believed **shamans** could communicate with the spirit world. They thought shamans used magic to control the weather and heal the sick. While shamans chanted prayers to the spirit world, other people played drums and danced.

Indian medicine men, or shamans, used to make medicine to help their people feel better. Do you think this is how medicine is made for you when you are sick?

Ceremonies

The Abenaki often held *ceremonies*, or special gatherings, for many different reasons. One was held at the end of the hunting season. Another was held in the spring when the sap began to seep out of the maple trees. Others were held in the spring when women planted seeds and in the fall when they harvested crops.

The people usually began and ended ceremonies with prayers of thanks for what the people had received. Stories, songs, dances, games, and large meals were part of many ceremonial *traditions*.

Abenaki ceremonies were held to celebrate many things. What kind of ceremony do you think is shown in the picture? Why do you think the man in the middle of the circle is standing up?

Vision Quest

An important ceremony in every Abenaki boy's life was the **vision quest**. If you were an Abenaki boy, you were sent in search of a spirit who would help you and guard you from danger throughout your life. After *fasting,* or not eating, for several days, you would leave your village. You would go into the woods or mountains alone and find a quiet spot and wait for your guardian spirit. Your guardian spirit would appear as an animal in a vision or dream.

Social Connections

The Abenaki shared common ideas about *social* things, such as work, spiritual beliefs, and family. Storytelling and games were other important things they shared.

Family Connections

Families were important to the Abenaki. Each family chose an animal to use as its family symbol.

The people took care of each other. Aunts and uncles watched over and guided young children. Older members of the village were respected and valued for their wisdom.

Parents rarely yelled at their children. If children needed to be punished, mothers and fathers told them stories that had *morals*. If the children behaved badly again, parents reminded them of the stories.

Storytelling

The people did not write down important things that happened to them. They told stories about those things. The stories were often *legends* that explained things about the tribe's history. They also taught children lessons that could help them later in life.

Stories were often about family members who lived long ago. Sometimes stories told of brave men who earned respect during war or while hunting. Many stories were about animals, weather, and the land.

Children worked hard to memorize each word of the stories they heard. Since stories were not written down, people with good memory skills were praised.

Children learned many things from the stories they heard. What things have you learned from stories?

Games

Games were important in Abenaki villages. They were a way for people to relax, have fun, and enjoy being together. Some games taught boys skills they needed for hunting or for protecting the tribe.

Abenaki invented the game of lacrosse. Like players today, the men played with netted sticks, a ball, and a field. The nets were rawhide baskets similar to fish nets. The ball was a piece of deerskin filled with moose hair and then tied into a bag. The sticks were often decorated.

The game field was a cleared meadow near the village. There was a goal at each end of the field. The entire village often played. Each side tried to get the ball into their goal to score a point.

There were no rules for behavior on the field. Players used arms, knees, feet, and sticks to get the ball. They were often hurt. Lacrosse was usually played for fun, but sometimes it helped settle arguments between two people.

Lacrosse means "the cross." The game was named by early French explorers who watched the Abenaki play. The stick reminded the Frenchmen of the cross shapes used in their churches. Lacrosse is still a popular sport today. How do you think it is different from the way it looks in this picture?

The people played a winter game called snow snake. Each player had a stick. One player at a time called out the name of his snow snake stick. Then he threw it as far as he could into a narrow ditch dug into the snow. After everyone had thrown his stick, the person whose stick went the farthest won the game. The winner gathered up the bundle of snow snakes and then threw them into the air. Other players scrambled to get their own stick back or to capture the stick they thought was the best.

Some snow snake sticks were highly decorated. Why do you think the Abenaki chose to decorate their snow snakes?

Connecting the Past with the Present

The Abenaki did not live only long ago. Many Abenaki live in New Hampshire today. They work and go to school in many communities. They are part of our modern culture, but they have a very special connection to the past.

Some modern Abenaki parents teach their children traditional customs and legends. They want to make sure the ways of their people are not forgotten over time. Why is it important to keep a connection to the past? What traditions do you have in your home that are passed down from your parents, grandparents, and great grandparents?

LESSON 3 KEY IDEA REVIEW

1. What did the Abenaki ceremonies consist of?
2. What was the job of a shaman?
3. Why did the Abenaki tell legends?

In what ways is this modern Abenaki girl keeping her traditions alive?

Go to the Source

A Seacoast Whale Artifact

This drawing shows an artifact that was discovered in Seacoast, New Hampshire. Archaeologists think it may have been used as a sinker weight to weigh down a fishing line. It may also have been some sort of religious totem that was held up by the hole in the tail of the fish. It is thought to have been carved from stone in the Late Archaic period of Native American culture that dates from 3,500 to 5,000 years ago.

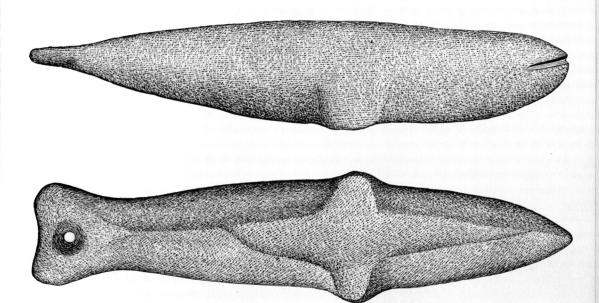

Go to the Source

LOOK	THINK	DECIDE
What does the artifact look like and what details make you think that?	Why do you think the artifact hasn't broken apart?	What would the people in the Late Archaic period have used to carve this?

CHAPTER REVIEW

Spotlighting Geography | Abenaki Tribes

Use the map on page 59 to answer the questions about the Abenaki tribes of New Hampshire.

1. Why do you think there aren't exact borders shown for each of the tribes?
2. Why is it important for tribes to live near rivers, lakes, and forests?
3. What type of food do you think the tribes along the rivers ate?
4. How many Abenaki tribes live in today's New Hampshire?

Becoming a Better Reader | Set a Purpose for Reading

Good readers always set a purpose for reading. Part of setting a purpose for reading is thinking about what you already know about a subject. Chapter 4 is about explorers and settlers. Create your own KWL chart to show what you know and what you want to know about New Hampshire's explorers and settlers. At the end of chapter 4, you will complete your chart by writing what you learned.

Reviewing the Big Idea

1. What is the name of the Indian tribe the explorers met?
2. Describe what the prehistoric times would have been like.
3. Develop a set of instructions telling how to build a wigwam.
4. How does the Abenaki's daily work differ from our daily work?
5. What would happen if the Abenaki did not remember their family legends?
6. Do you think lacrosse was a good or bad thing for the Abenaki to do?

Big Idea

How did European exploration change life in North America and lead to the colony of New Hampshire?

This picture shows colonists walking on a town street. How do you think the area looked before settlers built the town?

Timeline of Events

1000S
Vikings explore the coast of North America.

1603
Martin Pring explores the coast of Maine and New Hampshire.

1000

1500

1600

1492
Columbus lands on islands off the North American coast.

1606
King James of England claims the right to colonize American lands.

1500S
European explorers arrive in New England.

Explorers and Settlers

Early European explorers who visited New England returned to their countries with descriptions of woods, water, and wildlife. It seemed like the perfect place for European families to make a new home.

1614
Captain John Smith explores the New England coast.

1623
• David Thomson forms Pannaway Plantation.
• The Hilton brothers establish Dover.

1656
Eunice Cole is first tried on charges of witchcraft.

1689
A series of colonial wars between British, French, and Indians begins.

1620   1640   1660   1680

1622
The Council for New England grants land to Sir Fernando Gorges and John Mason.

1641
The four towns of New Hampshire become part of the Massachusetts Bay Colony.

1679
The king of England separates New Hampshire and Massachusetts.

1690
New Hampshire becomes part of Massachusetts once again.

1620
King James forms the Council for New England.

Key Idea

Why did Europeans begin to explore the New World?

Words to Understand

colony
discovery
explorer
export
import
merchant
waterway

What do you think this Native American woman was thinking when she saw this ship?

Changes on the Horizon

Imagine you are an Abenaki boy or girl standing on the shore of the Atlantic Ocean one morning. Along the horizon, you notice something unusual. At first, it looks like a small, dark object. But as it gets closer, it looks like a cloud floating just above the water.

A little while later, you realize the object is not a cloud. It is a large ship. It is much bigger than any boat you have ever seen before. You run to get the other people in your village.

By the time you return, small boats are lowered from the ship's sides. Men with light skin and hairy heads and faces row toward shore and climb out of their boats. They are wearing clothing you have never seen before. The men begin speaking in a language you have never heard. What should you do? How do you feel? You don't know where the men came from or why they have come. You don't know that your life and the lives of your people will change forever.

Explorers in the New World

The Abenaki had lived many years on the land we know as New Hampshire. They lived in harmony with nature. There was plenty of food, water, and wood for everyone.

Far away, across the Atlantic Ocean, another people lived in a place called Europe. Many people in European countries lived in crowded cities. Their forests had been cut down to build homes and businesses. There was not enough land or food for everyone. The *discovery* of a new world could help the Europeans find resources they needed.

Leaders of European countries hired *explorers* to travel the world in search of new sources of goods to support their growing populations. They also wanted to find new land for Europeans to live on.

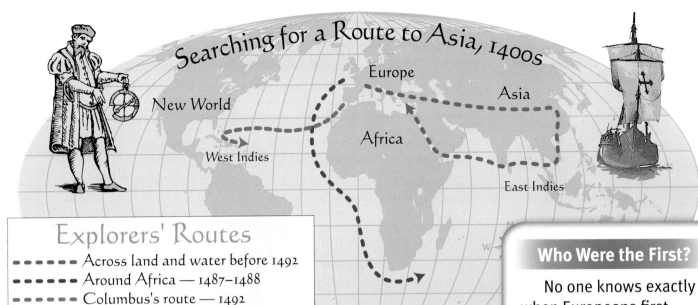

Searching for a Route to Asia, 1400s

New World
Europe
Asia
Africa
West Indies
East Indies

Explorers' Routes
- - - - - Across land and water before 1492
- - - - - Around Africa — 1487–1488
- - - - - Columbus's route — 1492

Explorers were also looking for new trade routes to China, India, and Japan. Europeans wanted to trade lumber, furs, and woolen cloth for Asian spices, jewels, and silk.

Christopher Columbus was a European sailor who was looking for a new trade route to Asia. When he landed on islands off North America's coast, he thought he had reached the East Indies. So he called the native people he met "Indians."

Christopher Columbus

The Importance of Trade

Different regions in the world have different natural resources. Asian countries didn't have the forests, furs, and fish found in North America. European countries didn't have spices and silk that Asian countries had. These goods were in high demand in each region. Many people wanted them. Trading these goods helped people in all these regions.

Europeans *exported,* or sent, timber and fur to Asia. They *imported,* or brought back, spices and silk.

Who Were the First?

No one knows exactly when Europeans first visited North America. Many archaeologists believe the first Europeans were Vikings. They discovered remains of a small Viking settlement on Newfoundland Island in Canada. The Vikings were sailors from the countries of Denmark, Norway, and Sweden. Archaeologists believe they explored the coast of North America about 500 years before Christopher Columbus arrived.

Look at a globe and find Europe. Now find North America and Asia. Are they close together? During Columbus's time, the journey from Europe to the Far East was long and dangerous. Merchants loaded goods onto ships and sailed across a big sea. The merchants and their goods had to survive bad weather, rough ocean voyages, and thieves during long months of travel. Then they unloaded the goods and took them overland by pack animals on a trail called the Silk Road. Once the goods were traded in Asia, the new items were taken by caravan and shipped back to Europe. Since moving the goods was so difficult, they were too expensive for most people to buy.

This is an artist's idea of the Silk Road. Do you think this is what the Silk Road really looked like?

European Explorers

Europeans were excited about the natural resources in North America. Wealthy ***merchants*** in Spain, France, and England sent ships to the New World. They wanted their traders to bring wood, furs, gold, and fish back to Europe. They needed wood to make ship masts, furs to make hats, and fish to feed people. Europeans found some gold in the New World but not in New Hampshire.

Europeans called the Americas the "New World" because it was new to them.

French Explorers

The French explored parts of Canada and the Mississippi River. They started towns on lands next to those settled by England. The French people learned the languages and culture of local Indian tribes. The Abenaki traded animal furs and fish with the French for things like blankets and pots.

English Explorers

England sent Martin Pring to explore the coast of New England. Pring was told to find a water route across North America and to look for sassafras trees. Sassafras was believed to cure colds and other common illnesses. Pring and his men sailed two ships up the Piscataqua River. They made maps of the *waterway* and New England's coastline.

Pring kept a journal of his travels. He described New Hampshire in this way: "Very goodly groves and woods . . . with tall oakes, beeches, pine-trees, hazels, and maples. We also saw sundry sorts of beasts: deere, beares, wolves, foxes. . . ."

Native American Point of View

There are no written records that describe the thoughts and feelings of Native Americans when they first met travelers from France and England. The closest we can get to understanding their points of view is through journals of European explorers and settlers. Most Europeans, like William Wood, reported that Native Americans were very kind to the new arrivals. "They are a loving people. Yet, are . . . very wary with whom they strike hands in friendship. . . ."

The Native Americans here are trading with French explorers. What items are being traded?

Creating Colonies

King James of England believed the cheapest way to get natural resources from the new land to Europe was to establish colonies in North America. A *colony* is a settlement under the control of a country far away. The king believed he had the right to start colonies here so he could gain wealth for his country.

Exploring the Northeast Coast

English merchants hired Captain John Smith to explore the northeast coast of North America. They hoped the region would be a good place to set up a colony. Earlier, Captain Smith had helped create a settlement in Virginia called Jamestown.

Captain Smith sailed around the Isles of Shoals and named the islands "Smith's Isles." He explored the coast and wrote descriptions of the region. He reported on the kindness of the native people. He believed the land would be a good place for English families to settle. He called the region New England.

This is a painting of John Smith's arrival in New England. The crew had been at sea for many weeks. What do you think the men thought of this new place?

THE WRITING OF JOHN SMITH

Captain John Smith wrote *A Description of New England*. In the book, he describes his journey along the New England coast. His book gave English readers details of a land filled with great beauty and resources.

Captain Smith describes thick forests, plentiful fish, and comfortable temperatures.

We saw . . . gardens and corn fields . . . strong and well proportioned people . . . a most excellent place. . . . And of all the four parts of the world that I have yet seen . . . I would rather live here than anywhere. . . .

Smith's book encouraged English families to leave their homelands and settle in North America. How were his travel descriptions similar to articles in today's travel magazines and newspapers? Why do you think the English families were willing to move to an unfamiliar place that they had only read about? Have you ever wanted to visit a place because of something you read?

New Hampshire
Inspirations

LESSON 1 KEY IDEA REVIEW

1. What were European explorers looking for?
2. How did the Native Americans treat the European explorers?
3. Where did John Smith explore?

LESSON ② New Hampshire Is Born

Key Idea

What was life like in the new English colony of New Hampshire?

Words to Understand

blacksmith
council
grant
industry
memorial
permanent
plantation

The New Hampshire Colony

After Captain Smith gave a good report of New England, King James started a group called the Council for New England. The **council's** job was to encourage men to move to New England. It gave land grants to men who agreed to go. A land **grant** gave a man a free piece of land to live on and farm.

The council granted a huge section of today's northern New England to John Mason and Sir Fernando Gorges. They were granted all the land between the Kennebec River in today's Maine and the Merrimack River in today's New Hampshire.

Mason and Gorges decided to divide their land grant. Gorges took the land that became part of the state of Maine. Mason took the rest of the land. Although he never visited the region, Mason named his land New Hampshire in honor of his home in Hampshire, England.

What Do You Think ❓

As soon as English explorers visited the land, they claimed most of it for England. But Native Americans did not believe anyone could own land. They felt land was for everyone to use and enjoy. How do you think Native Americans felt about Europeans claiming the land for themselves?

Pannaway Plantation

The Council for New England also granted land in today's New Hampshire to David Thomson and asked him to create a **plantation**, or large farm, near the Piscataqua River. They told him to grow crops, search for gold, trade with the natives, and fish.

Mason and Gorges decided to divide their land. What do you see written on this map?

JOHN MASON
1586–1635

Captain John Mason was born in England. He was a sailor, explorer, and government leader.

John became the governor of a colony in Newfoundland. He also drew the first known English map of the island. After he finished his term as governor, the king did not replace him. The colony was later abandoned.

John helped people leave England and settle in New Hampshire. He gave them supplies and tools to build homes and businesses in Strawbery Banke.

Shortly after the colonists arrived, other men in England claimed that some of John's land belonged to them. John died before the problem was solved. After his death, his family asked the English courts to declare the Mason family as New Hampshire's only landlord. The courts did not agree. The British government soon gave land grants to other people.

NEW HAMPSHIRE PORTRAIT

Thomson and a few men settled at Odiorne's Point (now part of Rye). The men built a house, a fort for trading with natives, and a blacksmith's shop (a **blacksmith** made tools from iron). They never found any gold.

Thomson named his settlement Pannaway Plantation. It became a fishing community, but it only lasted a few years. Most of the settlers moved north to the growing town of Strawbery Banke. David Thomson eventually moved to an island in Boston Harbor and built a home. Colonists then used the land at Pannaway to plant crops.

Settlement at Dover

In the same year that Thomson settled Pannaway Plantation, brothers Edward and William Hilton from London built a settlement at Hilton's Point. Today, we call this place Dover.

Not much is known about why the Hilton brothers started a settlement. Some historians believe they might have been part of Thomson's group and left to start their own community. Dover became our state's first *permanent* settlement. Today, it is one of our state's largest communities.

Colonists worked hard to build a settlement at Dover. What do you think the Hilton brothers did first to build the community?

Seacoast Settlements

Salt-marsh hay is a grasslike plant that grows in swampy areas. Farmers used it to feed their cows.

The first English settlements in the New Hampshire Colony were along the coast, which helped logging, fishing, and farming become big *industries* in the colony. Colonists could easily load their goods onto ships. The land farther inland was considered wilderness. Look at the charts to find out about the first coastal towns.

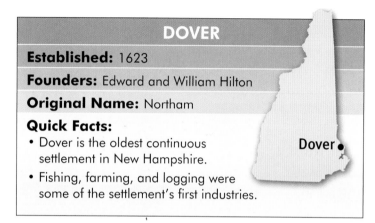

DOVER

Established: 1623

Founders: Edward and William Hilton

Original Name: Northam

Quick Facts:
- Dover is the oldest continuous settlement in New Hampshire.
- Fishing, farming, and logging were some of the settlement's first industries.

Dover

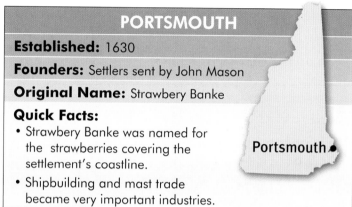

PORTSMOUTH

Established: 1630

Founders: Settlers sent by John Mason

Original Name: Strawbery Banke

Quick Facts:
- Strawbery Banke was named for the strawberries covering the settlement's coastline.
- Shipbuilding and mast trade became very important industries.

Portsmouth

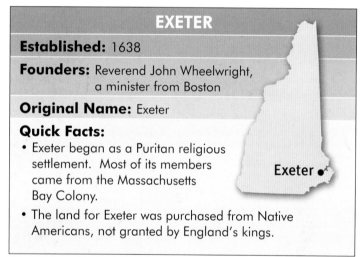

EXETER

Established: 1638

Founders: Reverend John Wheelwright, a minister from Boston

Original Name: Exeter

Quick Facts:
- Exeter began as a Puritan religious settlement. Most of its members came from the Massachusetts Bay Colony.
- The land for Exeter was purchased from Native Americans, not granted by England's kings.

Exeter

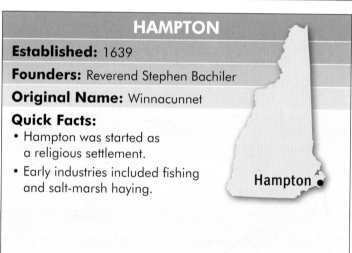

HAMPTON

Established: 1639

Founders: Reverend Stephen Bachiler

Original Name: Winnacunnet

Quick Facts:
- Hampton was started as a religious settlement.
- Early industries included fishing and salt-marsh haying.

Hampton

The Massachusetts Bay Colony

Puritans from England started the Massachusetts Bay Colony. They were led by a man named John Winthrop.

Puritans came to America to practice their religion freely. They had strong ideas about how life should be lived. Many Puritans settled in Exeter and Hampton. Rules for living in these towns were very strict.

New Hampshire
Massachusetts
Massachusetts Bay Colony

The King's Trees

One of the most important early industries in colonial New Hampshire was harvesting tall, thick pine trees for ship masts. Many people began calling the pines "mast trees."

England did not have tall, strong trees like those in New Hampshire. The British navy needed them for its ships. New Hampshire's trees became so valuable that the king ordered them to be saved for his navy's use.

He had the largest trees marked with an arrow symbol. Anyone who chopped down a marked tree without the king's permission was punished.

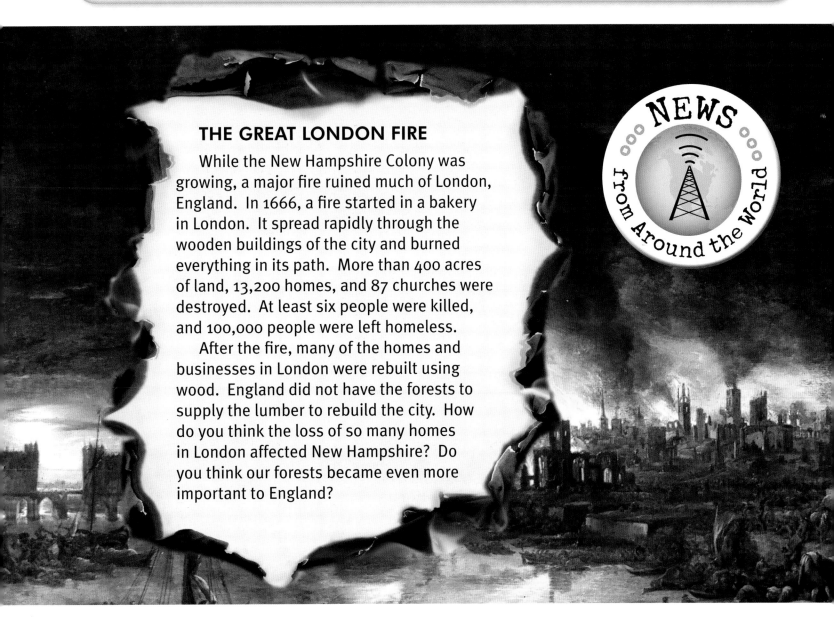

THE GREAT LONDON FIRE

While the New Hampshire Colony was growing, a major fire ruined much of London, England. In 1666, a fire started in a bakery in London. It spread rapidly through the wooden buildings of the city and burned everything in its path. More than 400 acres of land, 13,200 homes, and 87 churches were destroyed. At least six people were killed, and 100,000 people were left homeless.

After the fire, many of the homes and businesses in London were rebuilt using wood. England did not have the forests to supply the lumber to rebuild the city. How do you think the loss of so many homes in London affected New Hampshire? Do you think our forests became even more important to England?

NEWS from Around the World

WITCHCRAFT in the Colony

Imagine for a moment that you are in a tiny cabin with only a small fire to give you light and warmth. Outside, wilderness surrounds your home in every direction. Squawks, squeaks, and rustling sounds fill the dark night air.

Your fire gives you some comfort. But you keep thinking about your church minister's last sermon. The world is filled with evil, he warned.

The year is 1656. You live in a Puritan community in colonial New Hampshire. You must be careful about what you say and do. You must keep a watchful eye on your neighbors and family. Witches, your minister said, could be living in your community at this very moment.

It sounds like a spooky story told over a campfire, doesn't it? But in the 1600s, fear of witches was a very real part of many religions. People in Hampton were convinced a witch was living in their community.

Goody Cole

Goodwife Eunice Cole was not careful with her words. She always said what she thought. She did not act the way most people in Hampton thought she should. She stood trial many times for things she said to other people.

One day, Goody Cole's neighbors accused her of witchcraft. They claimed they had seen her turn into different animals. One man said that after his cattle grazed on Goody Cole's land, one of them died and another disappeared. Her neighbors took her to court, and she was found guilty of witchcraft.

Goody Cole was whipped and sent to prison in Boston. To pay for her food and care while she was there, the town of Hampton took everything she and her husband owned. After many years, she was released. She returned home to find her husband had died while she was gone.

Goody Cole was accused of witchcraft many more times and was sent back to jail for a few months.

A legend says that when Goody Cole died, the townspeople dragged her body into a pit. The exact location of her grave is unknown.

Three hundred years after her death, the town of Hampton placed an unmarked stone near the Tuck Museum. It is a memorial to Goody Cole. A *memorial* is something that reminds people of a person or an important event.

The name "Goody" was short for "Goodwife." It was a term of respect given to married women long ago.

The Witch Trials in Salem

Years after Goody Cole was accused of being a witch, hundreds of people in Massachusetts went to jail for the same crime. A special court was set up in Salem, Massachusetts, to hear witchcraft cases. Dozens of cases went before the court.

By the time the trials finally ended, 19 people in Massachusetts had been hanged as witches. Another person had been pressed to death with heavy stones. Countless others, like Goody Cole, had been forced to sit in damp, dark jails for months until the witch scare was over.

The people who were found guilty of witchcraft were not really witches. What do you think caused others to believe they were? Why do you think we don't have witch trials today?

Why Did They Come?

People who left Europe for New England in the 1600s did not know much about the land they went to settle. Most people did not know anyone who had traveled to New Hampshire. They did not know what their lives would be like.

Life was not easy for colonists when they arrived. Native Americans taught English colonists many things about hunting animals and planting crops. But even with help from native people, families struggled to survive. Colonists could not go to grocery stores to buy food. There were no factories to make fabric for clothes. For a while, there were no sawmills to cut trees into lumber for homes. Colonists had to do everything by hand. Providing a family with food, clothing, and shelter required long hours of work every day.

With so many hardships facing them, why did families come to New Hampshire? Why did they stay? Read these stories to find out:

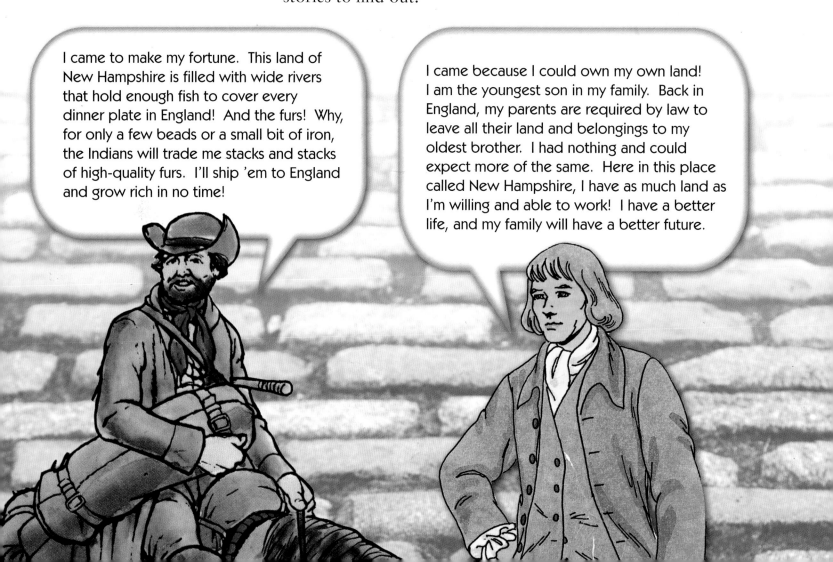

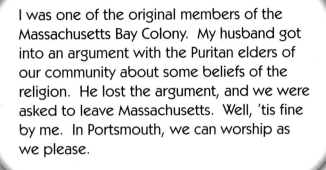

I was one of the original members of the Massachusetts Bay Colony. My husband got into an argument with the Puritan elders of our community about some beliefs of the religion. He lost the argument, and we were asked to leave Massachusetts. Well, 'tis fine by me. In Portsmouth, we can worship as we please.

These Puritans are being forced to leave Massachusetts. Why do you think they are not taking much with them? Where do you think they are going?

LESSON ② KEY IDEA REVIEW

1. Why were the first towns built along the Atlantic Coast?
2. What were the punishments for people found guilty of witchcraft?
3. List two reasons why people came to New Hampshire.

Key Idea

How did European settlers change the way the Abenaki lived?

Words to Understand

capture
convert
establish
immune
independent
monument
population
raid
revenge
treaty

New Hampshire as Part of Massachusetts

The first four settlements in New Hampshire were under the control of the king of England. But the towns did not work together to solve problems. Each town was *independent* of the others. Each made its own local rules and struggled to protect itself from Indian attacks.

The Massachusetts Bay Colony was very large and well organized, so the four small New Hampshire towns decided to become part of Massachusetts.

What clues in this picture show that the Massachusetts Bay Colony was well developed?

Changes in New Hampshire

Many important changes occurred when New Hampshire became part of Massachusetts:

- Inland areas were explored: Massachusetts leaders wanted to learn more about the wilderness sections of New Hampshire.

- More settlers arrived: Massachusetts granted New Hampshire land to many of its families. New Hampshire's *population* moved into inland areas.

- The first schools were *established:* Massachusetts passed a law requiring every town with 50 or more families to provide public education.

Fighting for Land

As settlers pushed deeper into New England's wilderness, they took land away from Native Americans. The colonists built towns on rivers where Indians fished, and they cut down trees in forests where Indians hunted for food.

Fighting between English settlers and Native Americans became frequent. Native people attacked English towns. English settlers attacked Indian villages. Many Abenaki leaders, like Passaconaway and his son, Wonalancet, tried to keep peace. But, finally, something happened that destroyed any good feelings between the New Hampshire native tribes and English settlers.

Native Americans and colonists fought many battles over land. Who do you think is winning this battle?

Many battles were fought over land between settlers and Native Americans. This illustration shows the "sham battle" area in Dover. What is the title of the picture? What kinds of things are happening?

Cocheco River

DOVER

Capture at Cocheco River

In 1675, Native Americans and colonists in southern New England began fighting each other. The war was called King Philip's War. King Philip was the chief of the Wampanoag people. One battle in Massachusetts was so terrible that hundreds of Indians fled to the Cocheco River near Dover. Soldiers from Massachusetts followed them.

Major Richard Waldron was in charge of the British settlement near Dover. He and the other settlers did not want the Indians to stay in New Hampshire. So Waldron created a plan to get rid of them. The settlers invited the Indians to come into town for a day of games. Hundreds of natives arrived for what they thought would be a day of fun.

After the Indians gathered, Massachusetts soldiers surrounded them. Within hours, more than 200 native men, women, and children were **captured** and forced to march to Boston. Some were hanged. Others were sold into slavery.

The name "King Philip" was given to the Native American chief by the English. One spelling of his Indian name was Metacom.

94

Deadly Revenge at Cocheco

The Indians did not forget what Major Waldron had done. They wanted *revenge*. A few years later, they attacked Dover, near the Cocheco River. They burned buildings, destroyed mills, and tore down homes. Major Waldron and 24 other settlers were killed. Many men, women, and children were taken prisoner and marched to French settlements in Canada to be sold or forced to work as servants.

This drawing shows the Indians' revenge on Major Waldron. Why do you think one of the Indians is sitting on the ground?

Kancamagus

Kancamagus was the grandson of Passaconaway. He was the last sachem of the Abenaki Pennacook tribe.

Kancamagus hated the English settlers and wanted them to leave. He led several *raids*, or attacks, against English settlers. He was both feared and respected by the English.

He was not successful in forcing the English to leave New Hampshire. Before his death, he signed a treaty with his English enemies. A *treaty* is a written agreement. In the treaty, England promised to punish any Englishman who harmed an Indian. The Native Americans promised to punish any Indian who harmed an Englishman. The treaty also promised that the two sides would protect each other from enemy attacks. But this peace did not last.

Today, Kancamagus is remembered in New Hampshire. The Kancamagus Highway and Mount Kancamagus both carry his name.

This is Kancamagus Highway. Do you think naming a highway after the Indian sachem was a good way to honor him?

What Do You Think ?

"**The oak will soon break before the whirlwind— it shivers and shakes even now. . . .**"
— *Passaconaway*

Passaconaway used things in nature to describe changes in Abenaki life after the arrival of Europeans. Why do you think he used an oak tree as a symbol for his way of life? What is he referring to when he talks about "the whirlwind"?

The Colonial Wars

For almost 200 years, England and France had been exploring and settling parts of North America. Both countries wanted to own more land.

In 1689, the first of four wars between England and France for control of North America took place. In the years that followed, many battles occurred in and near New Hampshire's towns and villages. Native American tribes helped both the English soldiers in New Hampshire and the French soldiers in Canada. During these colonial wars, the English, French, and Native Americans burned each other's homes and destroyed each other's crops. Hundreds of people died.

The Bravery of Hannah Duston

The Hannah Duston **monument** in Boscawen honors a brave woman who fought for her freedom during the colonial wars. Hannah was captured by Indians during a raid in Massachusetts and taken to New Hampshire. She escaped by killing 10 of her captors as they slept.

The monument to Hannah is meant to remind us of her courage. It is also a reminder about the terrible things that happen during times of war.

In this book, you will read about many battles in New Hampshire and the United States. As you learn about the dates, places, and reasons for the fighting, think about how wars changed people's daily lives. How are wars affecting the lives of American citizens today?

Changes for Native Americans

The early explorers brought things to give to and trade with the Native Americans. Missionaries brought European religions and worked to **convert** the natives to Christianity. But early visitors also brought something deadly to the Native Americans—diseases.

Over time, Europeans had become immune to many types of illnesses. If you are **immune** to something, your body has developed a way to fight it. Explorers did not know it, but they carried disease germs on their ships, clothes, and bodies.

Native Americans were not immune to European diseases. Smallpox, flu, and other deadly illnesses spread throughout native villages. Historians believe nearly all of the Native American population died from diseases brought by early European explorers.

The biggest change Europeans brought to Native Americans was disease. How would history be different if diseases had not killed nearly all of New England's Indians?

Cultures and Contact

Native Americans had their own traditions, customs, and ways of doing things. When the first Europeans visited New England, they brought their traditions and customs with them. The European way of life was very different from the Native American way of life.

How did the two cultures help each other in the early colonial years? How did the two cultures hurt each other? Which culture do you think benefited the most and why?

How does this Native American show things of Indian culture and European culture?

LESSON ③ KEY IDEA REVIEW 🔑

1. Why did New Hampshire join the Massachusetts Bay Colony?
2. Describe the capture of the Native Americans at Cocheco River.
3. Why did so many Native Americans die after the Europeans arrived?

Go to the Source

Study the French Axe Head

The French Axe Head is from the family of Hannah Duston. She took it when she escaped from an Abenaki family in 1697 near Concord.

LOOK

What can you tell about the axe head by looking at it?

THINK

How might the axe head have been helpful to Hannah Duston?

DECIDE

How does the axe head help us better understand this time in history?

Spotlighting Geography / Seacoast Settlements

The chart on page 86 shows where the first English settlements were in the New Hampshire Colony. Study the chart and answer the questions.

1. Where in New Hampshire were these towns settled?
2. Why were all the towns settled there?
3. What industries were started during this time?
4. How many years are there between the time Dover was settled and when Hampton was settled?

Reviewing the Big Idea

1. What did European explorers find in the New World?
2. What was the reason for the Salem witch trials?
3. Tell of a time when you had to meet someone new for the first time.
4. Compare the New World to New Hampshire today.
5. Give an alternate solution to the fight between the Native Americans and colonists.
6. Is the title of the chapter a good one or a poor one? Why?

Becoming a Better Reader / Making Connections

Good readers connect the text to themselves. They connect the text to things they already know or to personal experiences they have had. Use this strategy to make some connection with yourself and the text. Write a paragraph about a connection you had with this chapter. Perhaps you can write about a time when you explored something new and what you found there or about a time when you have stood up for something you believed in. Tell how your personal experiences connect with the text.

Big Idea

What was life like in the New Hampshire Colony?

This is a painting of colonial Exeter. What do you think colonial life would be like based on the painting?

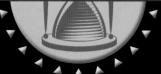

Timeline of Events

1713
The Indian Treaty of Portsmouth is signed.

1710   1720   1730

1717
John Wentworth is appointed royal lieutenant governor of the New Hampshire Colony.

1719
Scotch-Irish immigrants establish Londonderry.

Life in Colonial New Hampshire

Daily life in colonial New Hampshire was very difficult. Settlers worked hard to raise their families and make homes in their new world.

1741
- New Hampshire separates from Massachusetts.
- Benning Wentworth becomes royal governor of the New Hampshire Colony.

1763
Britain gains control of parts of Canada and land east of the Mississippi River.

1769
Dartmouth College is founded.

1740   1750   1760   1770

1754–1763
French and Indian War

1767
Sir John Wentworth becomes New Hampshire's royal governor.

Key Idea

How did life change during this time?

Words to Understand

architecture
flax
immigrant
replica
resign
slave
treaty

As the colony expanded, new towns were built, and older towns grew. What clues in this painting tell you that this colonial town is not new?

New Hampshire Colony Expands

In 1713, colonial leaders and Native American chiefs held a meeting to sign the Indian *Treaty* of Portsmouth. The treaty led to a period of peace between the two groups.

With less fear of Indian attacks, more Europeans from England, France, Ireland, and Scotland came to New Hampshire. Some came because they wanted to own their own land. Others came to make money by selling New Hampshire's natural resources. Many people simply wanted to live in a place where they had more control over the religions and laws that affected their lives.

The Native American chiefs who agreed to the Indian Treaty of Portsmouth signed it three times: with their French names, their English names, and their native names. Can you guess which ones are the native names?

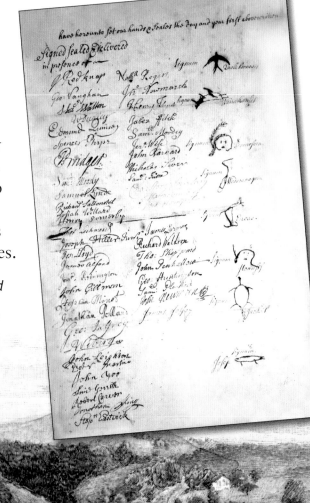

Scotch-Irish Settlers

Many *immigrants* traveled from Scotland and Ireland. They were known as Scotch-Irish. They started the town of Londonderry. Many Scotch-Irish immigrants were experts at growing potatoes and flax. Potatoes became an important source of food for the settlers. *Flax* is a long, thin plant. The Scotch-Irish settlers knew how to make flax into beautiful linen and lace fabrics.

Londonderry •

Flax

This is said to be a piece of the green silk from Mary's wedding dress. Do you believe the legend is true? Why or why not?

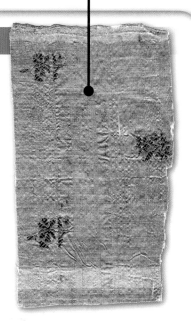

The Legend of Ocean-Born Mary

Do you know anyone who was born in a unique place? This legend is about a baby girl who was born on the ocean.

In 1720, James and Elizabeth Wilson left Ireland on a ship bound for New England. Elizabeth was soon going to have a baby. The Wilsons looked forward to raising their child in America, where the family would have new opportunities and a chance to own land.

Elizabeth gave birth to a beautiful girl on July 28, 1720, just as the ship was nearing Boston Harbor. Later that day, according to legend, pirates attacked the ship. The pirate captain told the frightened passengers he would not harm them if he was allowed to name the Wilsons' baby. He named her Mary. Some people believe Mary was the name of the pirate captain's wife. Others say it was his mother's name. The pirate captain gave the Wilsons a beautiful piece of green silk fabric for Mary to use for her wedding gown when she married. Then he and his pirates left in their ship without harming any passengers.

When ocean-born Mary and her family arrived in New Hampshire, they settled in Londonderry. Mary grew up and married a man named James Wallace. According to legend, she wore a wedding gown made from the pirate's green silk.

Slavery

Not everyone coming to New Hampshire did so of their own free will. Many were forced to come here. Many men, women, and children were captured on the west coast of Africa and brought to America on ships to live and work as slaves. A **slave** is someone who is owned by another person and forced to work without pay or freedom.

The sea journey between the African coast and North America was called the Middle Passage. The journey took several months. Hundreds of Africans were chained into the bottoms of ships. They were so tightly packed that most could not stand or stretch out their bodies. Many people died from diseases. When the ships arrived in American ports, the people were sold as slaves to wealthy colonists. Others were traded for rum or molasses.

New Hampshire did not have as many slaves as other colonies. But slavery existed here for more than 200 years. Enslaved people were forced to work on ships, on farms, and in the homes of many wealthy New Hampshire families.

Enslaved people wore chains like these while on the Middle Passage.

This map shows how the slave trade worked. Follow the triangle to see where the goods and enslaved people were traded. Where did sugar and molasses come from?

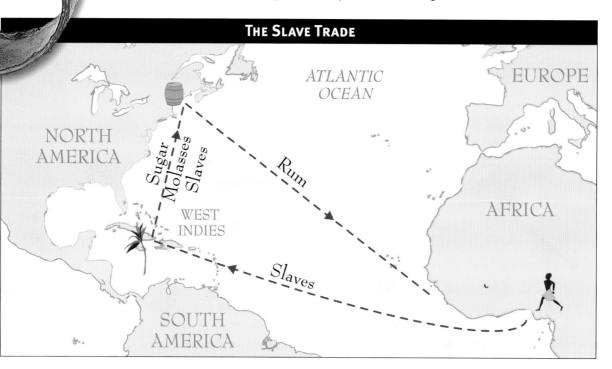

THE SLAVE TRADE

ATLANTIC OCEAN

EUROPE

NORTH AMERICA

Sugar Molasses Slaves

Rum

WEST INDIES

AFRICA

Slaves

SOUTH AMERICA

This large slaving boat is being chased by a smaller boat with men in blue uniforms. Why do you think they are trying to catch the large boat?

NEWS from Around the World

THE CITY OF NEW ORLEANS

While English settlers were colonizing New Hampshire, French settlers were establishing communities in other parts of North America.

In 1718, the French started the city of New Orleans in their colony of Louisiana. The site for New Orleans was chosen because it was surrounded by water. Goods could be transported on the water for trade.

Although New Orleans was claimed and governed by France, the settlement was also home to Native American and African families. These three groups of people brought their customs, traditions, languages, arts, clothing, and beliefs to New Orleans. The settlement became a blend of many cultures.

New Orleans

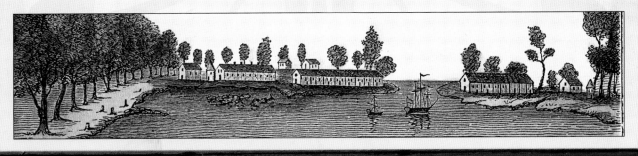

Today, there is a living history museum in Portsmouth called Strawbery Banke. Many of the houses at the museum were built in colonial days. Have you ever been there?

Charlestown • Strawbery Banke •

Growing Towns

As New Hampshire's population grew, many of its towns did as well. Life in the eastern region of the colony was different in many ways than life in the western region.

Strawbery Banke

Portsmouth was originally called Strawbery Banke. It became one of the fastest-growing and wealthiest towns in New England. People from all over the colony visited the town to buy goods brought from other countries to Portsmouth's harbor.

Historians study the *architecture* of Strawbery Banke's old buildings to learn how people in colonial times lived. The architecture helps historians answer questions about materials used for building and how items such as fireplaces were used. Actors at Strawbery Banke can tell you more about the houses and about living in Portsmouth during colonial times.

Fort at Number 4

The Massachusetts Bay Colony gave many land grants to settlers along New Hampshire's section of the Connecticut River. One of these grants was called Township Number 4. It was the northernmost English settlement in the 1740s and 1750s. Several families lived there during the colonial wars. They built a fort to protect themselves from attacks by the French and Indians. During one battle there, 31 English settlers fought hundreds of French soldiers and Indian warriors for three days. The French and Indians finally gave up and returned to Canada, but they continued to attack the fort for many years.

You can visit a **replica** of the Fort at Number 4 in Charlestown. Guides there will show you how colonists made clothes, prepared food, played games, and used the Connecticut River.

This is the replica of Fort at Number 4. If you visit, you can see how colonists used to live. What are all of the buildings made out of? Why do you think the colonists used this material to build the fort?

Separation from Massachusetts

New Hampshire had been part of the Massachusetts Bay Colony since 1690. But many residents began to think that leaders in Massachusetts did not know what was best for New Hampshire. They wanted to make their own decisions. They convinced the king to separate the two colonies in 1741. Benning Wentworth became New Hampshire's first royal governor.

BENNING WENTWORTH
1696–1770

Benning Wentworth was born in Portsmouth. He was the oldest of John Wentworth's 14 children. After he graduated from Harvard College in Massachusetts, he became a merchant in Portsmouth.

When King George II separated New Hampshire and Massachusetts, he appointed Benning as New Hampshire's first royal governor. Benning lived a life of luxury. He built a huge mansion in Portsmouth and held grand parties. But even though he spent a lot of money on himself, he did a lot to help the colonists.

Benning was the royal governor for more than 25 years. During that time, he issued hundreds of land grants for new towns in New Hampshire and what is now Vermont. He hired workers to build roads. He helped establish a stagecoach route between Boston and Portsmouth.

After many years, leaders in England began to distrust Benning. They believed some of his business deals were dishonest. Benning was forced to *resign,* or give up, his position as royal governor. He was replaced by his nephew, John.

LESSON ① KEY IDEA REVIEW

1. Why did people move to New Hampshire?
2. Where did enslaved people work?
3. Why did New Hampshire separate from Massachusetts?

Colonial Life

New Hampshire families worked hard to survive in colonial times. They built their own homes, grew their own food, made their own clothing, and established communities. Some colonists set up churches. Others organized schools. Many started small businesses. Living in communities like towns and villages, colonists were able to solve problems together, trade labor skills, educate their children, and protect themselves in times of war.

Key Idea

How does a colonial community differ from your community?

Words to Understand

apprentice
barter
fife
harpsichord
herb
quill
tavern

This colonial couple is standing outside a farmhouse. What clues can you find that tell you they are getting ready to work?

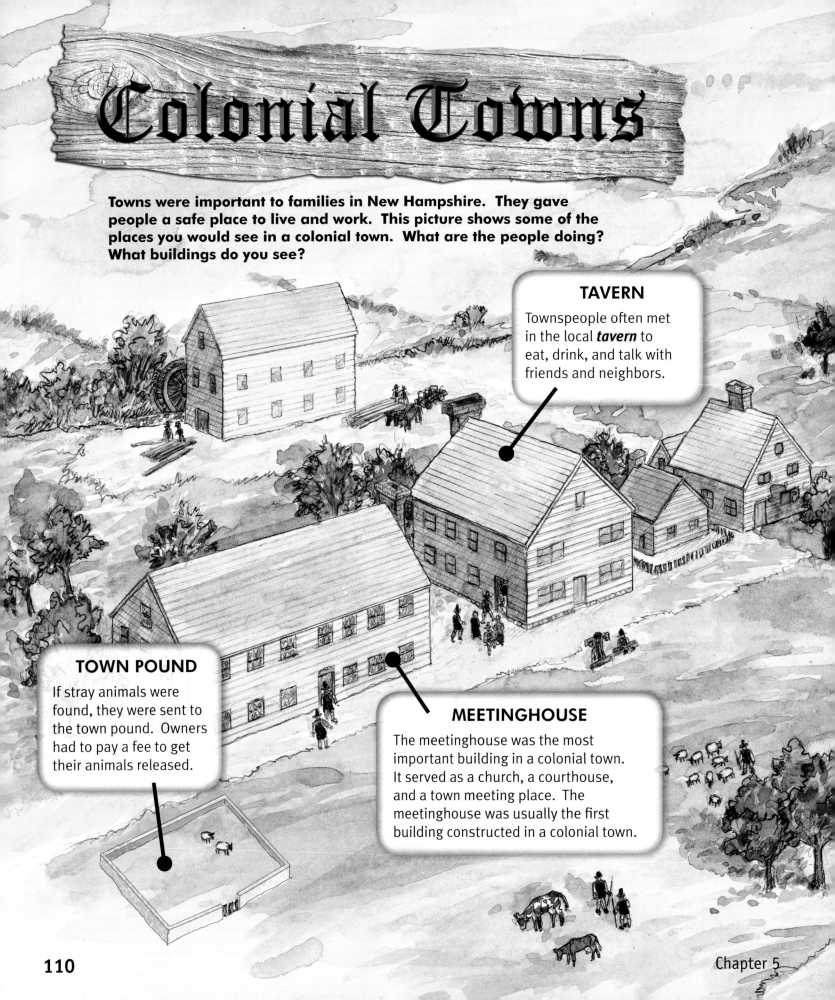

Colonial Towns

Towns were important to families in New Hampshire. They gave people a safe place to live and work. This picture shows some of the places you would see in a colonial town. What are the people doing? What buildings do you see?

TAVERN
Townspeople often met in the local *tavern* to eat, drink, and talk with friends and neighbors.

TOWN POUND
If stray animals were found, they were sent to the town pound. Owners had to pay a fee to get their animals released.

MEETINGHOUSE
The meetinghouse was the most important building in a colonial town. It served as a church, a courthouse, and a town meeting place. The meetinghouse was usually the first building constructed in a colonial town.

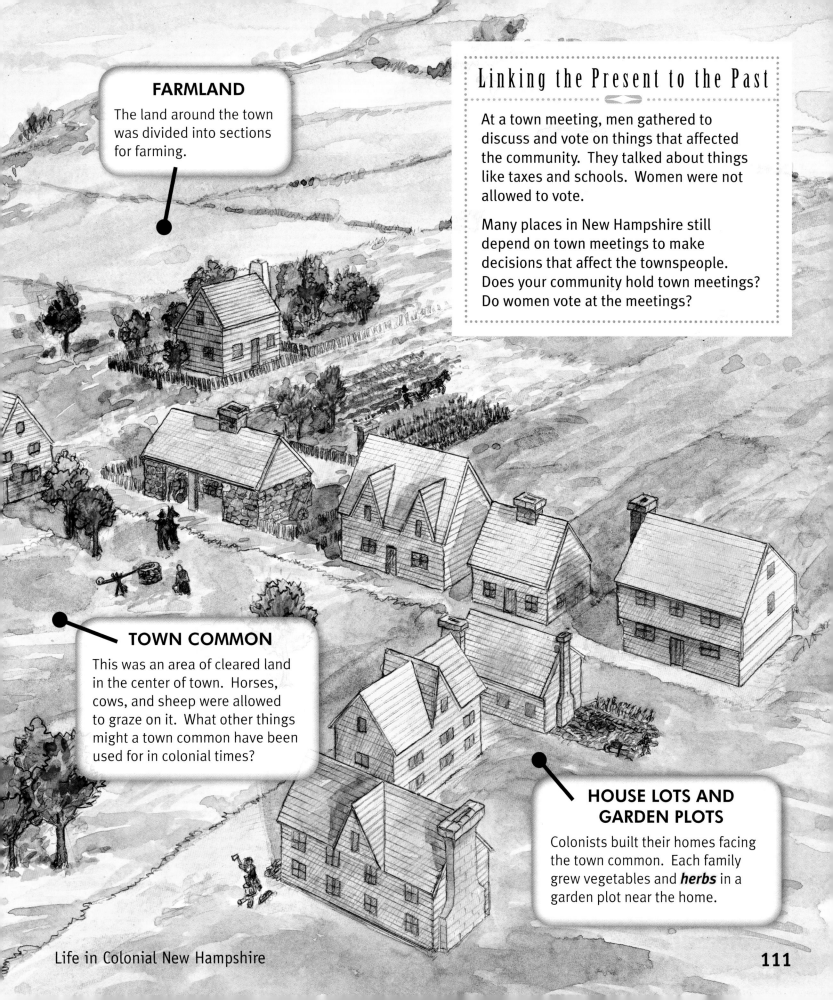

FARMLAND

The land around the town was divided into sections for farming.

Linking the Present to the Past

At a town meeting, men gathered to discuss and vote on things that affected the community. They talked about things like taxes and schools. Women were not allowed to vote.

Many places in New Hampshire still depend on town meetings to make decisions that affect the townspeople. Does your community hold town meetings? Do women vote at the meetings?

TOWN COMMON

This was an area of cleared land in the center of town. Horses, cows, and sheep were allowed to graze on it. What other things might a town common have been used for in colonial times?

HOUSE LOTS AND GARDEN PLOTS

Colonists built their homes facing the town common. Each family grew vegetables and *herbs* in a garden plot near the home.

Earning a Living

People had many different kinds of jobs in colonial times. Most men were farmers. Most farmers were also tradesmen. They traded things they made for things they needed. This is called **bartering.**

Farmers

Today, you might have packed your own lunch, or maybe you brought money to buy lunch. Did you have to grow your lunch yourself? Did you have to hunt it? Of course not! We have grocery stores that provide us with the food we need.

Colonists did not go to a grocery store to buy their food. They had to hunt or grow it. Boys helped their fathers chop down trees to make room for gardens. Girls planted seeds. Boys and girls both pulled weeds and harvested vegetables and herbs.

Harvesting crops was a lot of work in colonial days. It was all done by hand. Why do you think there is a baby in this picture?

Tradesmen

Tradesmen had special skills. They made things the community needed. Cobblers cut and sewed pieces of leather to make shoes. Millers used waterwheels or windmills to

Cobbler

Miller

Cooper

turn big stones that ground corn and wheat into cornmeal and flour. Coopers fit pieces of wood together to make barrels. Tanners dried and stretched animal skins into leather. Blacksmiths pounded iron into tools. Spinners spun wool or flax into yarn. Large towns had workers who cut lumber, dyed cloth, and built carriages. They also had gunsmiths, tinsmiths, silversmiths, and clock makers. Coastal towns had men who earned their livings by building ships.

Merchants

Merchants were businessmen who owned and ran general stores. At the general stores, colonists traded things like furs, crops, and clothing for things they needed, such as sugar and farm tools. Wealthy merchants bought ships and sailed their goods between the colonies and Europe, Africa, and the West Indies.

Apprentices

Tradesmen often hired *apprentices* to help them with their work. Boys could become apprentices to blacksmiths, printers, furniture makers, and other skilled craftsmen. Girls could be apprenticed to expert seamstresses or weavers.

Activity — A Job For You

If you lived during colonial times, which job would you choose? Make a prop or a drawing of the job you choose. For example, if you chose a blacksmith, you could make a hammer out of cardboard, or you could draw a picture of yourself making something out of metal.

Keep your job a secret, and take turns as a class showing each other your prop or drawing. Try to guess each other's jobs.

Tanner

Blacksmith

Spinner

Colonial churches were not heated. Some people brought small, metal boxes filled with hot coals to place between their feet. Others brought dogs to lie across their feet.

Pay Attention!

Each church had a tithing-man. He made sure everyone paid attention during the long sermons. He carried a pole as he walked up and down the church aisle. The tithing-man used the pole to tap the heads of children who made noise in church. One end of the pole had a feather or a squirrel's tale attached to it. The tithing-man used it to tickle the noses of adults who fell asleep.

Church in the Colony

In Puritan towns, people devoted Sunday to thinking about God and giving thanks. Sermons and prayers lasted most of the day. No one was allowed to work or play. In many towns, it was against the law not to attend church services.

Sunday Sermons

Each person in town had an assigned seat in church. Church officials sat in front. Men sat on one side of the main aisle. Women and girls sat on the other side. Boys sat in the back of the church.

The minister used stories from the Bible to teach people how to live good lives. He warned them of God's anger if they did not obey God. He spoke of the devil and evil. He taught the people about the power of witches. The minister's sermon was always very serious and sometimes even scary.

What Do You Think?

Why do you think men, women, and children sat separately in church? Why do you think the boys sat in the very back?

Colonial Homes

Imagine you are a colonial boy or girl. Your home is not very big. It is made of wood. Your father and uncles cut down many trees to build it. Your home does not have running water, gas, electricity, or an indoor bathroom.

Your home has one large room called a common room. It is your family's kitchen, living room, and bedroom.

There is a large fireplace in the common room. On cold nights, your family gathers around the fireplace to get warm. Your mother also uses the fireplace to cook the family's meals.

This colonial kitchen probably looks a lot different from your kitchen. What are the biggest differences? Look carefully at the picture and see if you can figure out what everything is.

Colonial homes didn't have glass windows. Women attached paper soaked in cooking grease to the window frames. The grease made the paper see-through.

As families grew, men built onto the backs of their houses. Houses like the one in the drawing were called saltbox houses because they looked like the boxes where salt was stored.

Colonial Families

Colonial families worked hard to get the food, clothing, and tools they needed. Pretend once again that you are a colonial child. Your mother spends long hours preparing food and making clothing. She boils huge pots of animal fat to make soap and candles. Your father clears fields and plants crops. He hunts and fishes. Your parents smoke and salt the meat to save it for later. If your family needs something it cannot make, your parents trade with other families.

Women worked hard to prepare each meal. Cooking usually took most of the day. What foods do you recognize in this picture?

What's for Dinner?

Your meals are cooked in fireplaces. The women in your family make stews in large kettles. They bake bread in iron kettles called Dutch ovens. They place hot coals underneath and on top of the Dutch ovens to cook the dough inside.

Native Americans taught your family many things about growing and preparing food. They showed you how to plant corn, beans, and squash and how to use the vegetables to cook succotash and corn bread.

In the 17th century, people ate from wooden bowls called trenchers. Usually, two or more people shared one trencher. By the 18th century, most people used pewter bowls and cups. Pewter is a metal made from copper and tin.

Colonists used oil from whale blubber to light homes and businesses. Whale blubber is fat. When it is heated, it melts into oil.

Colonial sailors caught whales off the coast of New England. They dragged the huge creatures to shore and cut out the blubber. By the late 18th century, the demand for whale oil had grown. New Englanders designed ways to boil the blubber right on the decks of large wooden ships. It was a very messy job!

Making Clothes

In your colonial family, your mother and sisters make all your family's clothing from sheep wool or flax. Flax takes a long time to grow. It takes many months to make a single shirt from a new flax plant. Your mother must grow the flax and then harvest it, clean it, spin it into thread, dye it, and weave it into cloth. Then she can cut the fabric and sew it into clothes.

SIR JOHN WENTWORTH
1737–1820

One governor did his best to make colonial life easier for families. His name was John Wentworth. He was born in Portsmouth into a powerful family. When he was 14, he entered Harvard College. By the time John was 29 years old, he was appointed royal lieutenant governor of New Hampshire.

As the last royal governor of the colony, John did many things to improve life for colonists. He ordered the building of roads, published the first accurate map of the colony, and made it easier for people to get land in New Hampshire's inner region. He even gave a large land grant to Reverend Eleazar Wheelock to build Dartmouth College in Hanover.

John was governor when the colonists decided to fight against Great Britain in the American Revolution. But John remained loyal to the king of England. He did not want the colonies to break away from Great Britain. In the months before the war, John and his family fled to Canada.

Colonial Education

Many young boys and girls attended school in their teacher's home. Parents often paid the teacher with eggs, corn, or other items instead of money.

Colonial children were expected to learn the alphabet so they could read the Bible. They used a hornbook to learn the alphabet. A hornbook was not really a book. It was a piece of wood with a sheet of paper that had the alphabet and the Lord's Prayer or a Bible verse printed on it. A thin sheet of clear animal horn protected the paper.

Colonial children wrote by dipping a goose feather, or *quill*, into a jar of homemade ink. They could only write a few words before they had to dip their pens into the ink again.

Education for Older Boys and Girls

After children learned to read simple words and phrases, girls finished their education with their mothers. They learned to cook, sew, and clean. Boys sometimes attended another school that prepared them for college or taught them how to become religious leaders.

This hornbook was used to teach school lessons. Can you tell what the lessons were about by reading the hornbook?

The earliest record of a New Hampshire teacher tells of John Legat of Exeter. He was hired in 1649 to teach reading and writing to all children in Hampton. His contract stated he was to be paid in corn, cattle, and butter.

Older boys used The New England Primer. *This was a small textbook used for more than 100 years. It taught the alphabet, spelling lessons, and pages of Bible verses. How is it different from your textbook?*

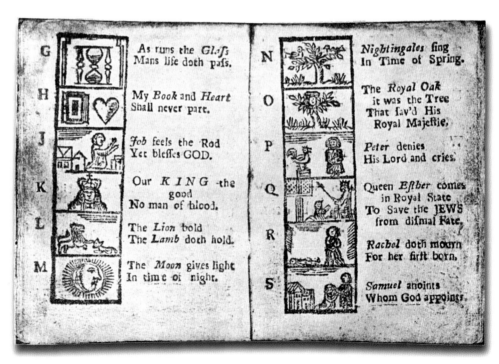

Dartmouth College

Dartmouth College in Hanover was the first college in New Hampshire. It was founded by Reverend Eleazar Wheelock. The British government planned to use Dartmouth to teach Indian tribes and English children. The first class had only four students.

Dartmouth College is still open today. Many famous people have attended the school. A few well-known students were Daniel Webster, Robert Frost, and Theodor "Dr. Seuss" Geisel.

New Hampshire Inspirations

COLONIAL CREATIVITY

Do you like to paint pictures or draw? Do you enjoy dance classes or writing poetry? Most colonists did not have the time or money to create art simply for fun. Instead, they created art while they worked.

Men built wooden furniture. They often carved beautiful designs of flowers and leaves into chairs and benches. Women stitched special designs into quilts. They gave the quilts as gifts on special occasions, such as a wedding or the birth of a baby.

Girls stitched art into samplers. A sampler was a piece of fabric on which a girl sewed tiny pictures of trees, flowers, and letters of the alphabet. As she worked, the girl learned different stitches and perfected her sewing skills.

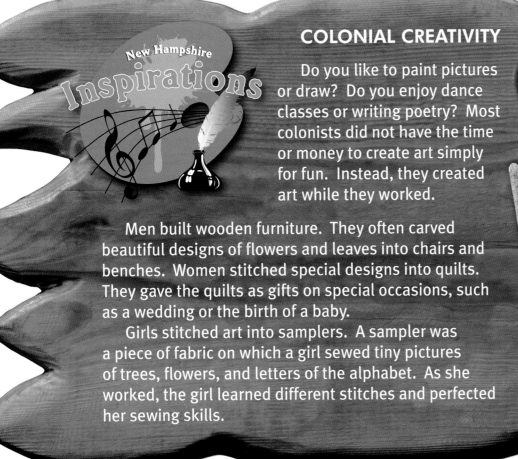

This is a portrait of Benning Wentworth. Answer the questions to see if you can learn more about Wentworth from the portrait.

1. What do you notice about his clothes? What kinds of activities do you think he did in these clothes?
2. What does Wentworth's expression tell you about his character?
3. What is the setting of this painting? What objects are in the room?
4. Why do you think this painting was made?

Colonial Music

Music was an important part of colonial life. It was a fun way for families and community members to enjoy time with one another. Violins, fiddles, and flutes were the most popular instruments. Men played *fifes*, recorders, and German flutes. Wealthy women often played *harpsichords* and English guitars.

Fifers and drummers were important in colonial militaries. They played during parades, marches, and battles, and in soldiers' camps to call the men to duty.

Even with all the hard work colonists had to do just to survive, they still took time to play music together with instruments like these. Is music important to you? Why or why not? Can you name each of the instruments in this drawing?

The game of hoop roll was fun for all ages. Players used a stick to roll a metal or wooden hoop along the ground. Children often raced each other as they rolled their hoops. Does this game look like fun to you?

Colonial Games

Colonial children found time to play after they finished their chores. Girls made dolls from corn husks. Boys carved whistles or spinning tops from wood scraps. Thin tree trunks became walking stilts. Riverbank clay was rolled into marbles.

Have you ever played jacks? Colonial children played jacks, too. They called the game "jackstones." Instead of metal jacks, they used small stones or pumpkin seeds. Instead of a bouncy ball, they tossed a stone into the air.

Many games played by colonial children are still played today. Which ones have you played?

- hide-and-seek
- tug-of-war
- leapfrog
- jump rope
- hopscotch
- checkers
- tag

LESSON 2 KEY IDEA REVIEW

1. What was a colonial home like?
2. What are two household jobs colonial women did?
3. How was a colonial child's education different from your education?

Key Idea

What was the cause of the French and Indian War?

Words to Understand

captive
declare
defend
ransom
savage
trader

This painting shows the Battle of Rogers' Rock. This fight is also known as the Second Battle on Snowshoes. Why do you think it is called that?

The French and Indian War

One thing that made life for English colonists very difficult was problems with the French and the Indians. After many colonial battles, the problems erupted into the French and Indian War.

British soldiers and explorers wanted to settle more lands, so they began pushing farther west. But French *traders* and families living on those lands did not want British settlers to take away the land they had settled.

Native Americans also lived on the land claimed by the British and French, and they wanted to keep the land for themselves. They knew they could not win a fight against both countries. Some Native Americans agreed to help the French if war started. Others agreed to help the British.

War Begins

Major General Edward Braddock was the commander of the British forces. A young soldier named George Washington was assigned to help him.

After several battles, war between Britain and France was officially *declared* in 1756. For the next seven years, the European enemies fought for control of North America. Fort at Number 4 in Charlestown served as a station for troops from the New England colonies.

Rogers' Rangers

Captain Robert Rogers led a group of men called Rogers' Rangers in attacks on Indians near Quebec. He wanted to help the British win control of New England and Canada.

Most of Captain Rogers' men were New England farmers. He trained them to move quietly through the woods and to fight. In one famous battle, the Rangers made a surprise attack on an Indian village in Canada. They killed many people, including women and children.

Heroes?

After the attack on the Indian village, Rogers' Rangers were seen as heroes by English settlers. People often fight wars to take power away from those who do not share their points of view. People also fight wars to *defend* something.

Robert Rogers

Britain Takes Control

After many long years of fighting, the war ended. The British won almost all of the French territory in Canada and most of the land east of the Mississippi River. Many Native American families left New England and moved to Canada in search of peace.

What Do You Think

Do you think Native Americans saw Rogers' Rangers as heroes? Why or why not?

These are actors playing soldiers in the French and Indian War. Notice how clean their uniforms are. Do you think this is really what soldiers looked like during battle?

Susanna Johnson
Indian Captive

During the colonial wars and the French and Indian War, Native Americans captured many British settlers and marched them to French settlements in Canada. They took many *captives* to replace family members who had died in battle or from sickness. Some prisoners were *ransomed* in exchange for money. One of New Hampshire's most famous captives was Mrs. Susanna Johnson.

Early one morning, Indians stormed the Johnson home in Charlestown. They captured Susanna and her family and marched the captives more than 150 miles over mountains and across lakes and rivers to Canada. Susanna gave birth to Elizabeth Captive Johnson along the way. Read the following entry in Susanna's diary to learn her amazing story of survival and courage.

August 30, 1754

In an instant a crown of savages (natives) . . . rushed furiously in. . . . I was led to the door fainting and trembling . . . my three little children were driven naked to the place where I stood. . . . Two savages laid hold of each of my arms and hurried me through thorny thickets. . . .

At the distance of three miles there was a general halt. The savages . . . gave us a loaf of bread, some raisins and apples which they had taken from the house. . . . By this time my legs and feet were covered with blood . . . and the Indians gave me a pair of moccasins . . . not one of our savage masters could understand a word of English.

They were eleven in number; all men of middle age, except one, a youth of sixteen . . . . [My] eldest [child] Sylvanus was but six years old. My sister Miriam was fourteen. My husband was barefoot and otherwise thinly clad. My two daughters had nothing on but their shifts and I had only the gown handed to me by the savages.

We went six or eight miles and stopped for the night. My sister . . . must lie between two Indians with a cord thrown over her and passing under each of them. . . . The Indians observed great silence and never spoke but when necessary. My children were much more peaceable than could be imagined. Gloomy fear imposed a deadly silence.

Is Susanna's journal a primary or secondary source? In this journal entry, she tells what happened when her family was captured. You learn of the events from her point of view. What if something in the story was changed? How would things have been different? Talk with your classmates about how this story would be different if the Johnson family and the natives spoke the same language. Now talk about how the story would be different if everyone but Susanna had been captured that night.

Susanna was probably used to hard work. How do you think that helped her survive her capture and her journey to Canada?

LESSON ③ KEY IDEA REVIEW

1. Why was the French and Indian War started?
2. Which country gained control of most of North America after the war?
3. Who was Susanna Johnson?

Go to the Source

Portraits of Woodbury and Sarah Langdon

John Singleton Copley painted these portraits during the colonial period. The portraits are of husband and wife, Woodbury and Sarah Langdon. Woodbury was known as remarkably good-looking. He was also considered shrewd, haughty, and sarcastic. Sarah was known as one of the fairest creatures who ever stepped out of a Portsmouth doorway. Study the portraits and answer the questions.

Go to the Source

LOOK

What can you tell about the Langdons by looking at their clothing?

THINK

Why do you think they had their portraits painted?

DECIDE

Do you think these portraits represent life for most people in New Hampshire at the time?

Spotlighting Geography | The Slave Trade

The map on page 104 shows the route of the slave trade. Study the map and answer the questions.

1. What three continents were part of the slave trade?
2. What ocean was used for the slave trade?
3. What was traded using this route?
4. Where were the slaves taken before sailing to North America?

Reviewing the Big Idea

1. List the different jobs colonial men did.
2. Why were Africans forced to move to New Hampshire?
3. How is your life different from the life of a colonial child?
4. What was a colonial community like?
5. Summarize the French and Indian War.
6. How did the French and Indian War affect the people?

Becoming a Better Reader | Visualize the Text

Good readers "see" the story in their heads as they read. It's like going to the movies in your head every time you open a book. Picturing the story in your head helps you make the connections needed to understand. We call this reading strategy visualizing the text. *New Hampshire, Our Home* is full of stories of exciting people and events. Choose a person, event, or way of living from this chapter to describe or retell in your own words. Be sure to use your senses to provide some of the details.

How did the American Revolution change life in North America and in New Hampshire?

New Hampshire in the American Revolution

This is a painting of the Battle of Bunker Hill. Many men from New Hampshire fought in this battle. They were led by Colonel Stark. Why do you think the man in front is holding a sword?

Timeline of Events

1770
Boston Massacre

1775 —
• (April) Battles of Lexington and Concord
• (June) Battle of Bunker Hill

1776
• New Hampshire leaders write a state constitution.
• The Declaration of Independence is approved.

1770   1775

1773 —
Boston Tea Party

1774
• The First Continental Congress meets in Philadelphia.
• Colonists raid Fort William and Mary.
• New Hampshire declares independence from Great Britain.

New Hampshire played an important role in the American Revolution. At town meetings, at busy shipping ports, and on faraway battlefields, New Hampshire's people fought for liberty from British rule.

1784
New Hampshire adopts the current state constitution and elects its first governor.

1779
Slaves in New Hampshire petition the new state legislature for freedom.

1787
The U.S. Constitution is written and adopted.

1780

1785

1790

1775–1783
American Revolution

1783
The Treaty of Paris is signed.

1788
New Hampshire ratifies the U.S. Constitution.

Key Idea

Why did the colonies rebel against Britain?

Words to Understand

congress
cooperation
Loyalist
massacre
Patriot
rebel
representative
revolution
surrender
tax

These playing cards have been stamped to show they have been taxed. What words can you read on the stamp?

Troubles with Britain

By the 1760s, Great Britain had many colonies in North America. King George wanted the colonists to pay back the money his country had spent on the French and Indian War.

He taxed many things the colonists bought from Great Britain, such as sugar, molasses, glass, paper, paint, and tea. A **tax** is money people must pay to a government.

One of the new taxes was the Stamp Act. Certain types of paper, like personal letters and daily newspapers, had to have special stamps on them. Colonists had to pay for the special stamps.

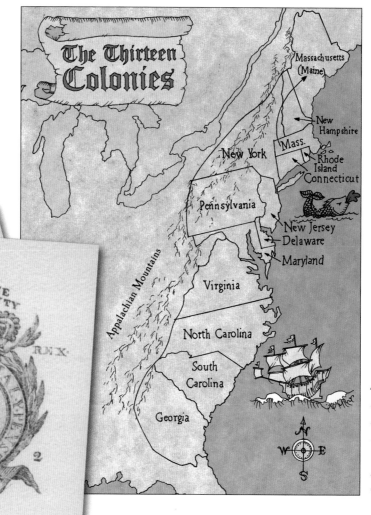

Although Britain had many colonies in North America, the "13 colonies" were those that rebelled against Great Britain.

No More Taxes!

The colonists didn't think it was fair for Britain to tax them on the things they used every day. They wanted to make their own decisions about taxes and other laws instead of following British rules. Some people wanted to send *representatives* to Britain to help make laws. But the king said no.

Many colonists were angry. Their motto became "No taxation without representation!" They *rebelled,* or went against, the stamp tax. The colonists also refused to buy tea, sugar, cloth, and other items from British merchants.

King George thought the colonists were getting out of control, so he sent soldiers to Boston to keep the peace. The soldiers stayed in many colonists' homes without permission.

Unrest in New Hampshire

Settlers in New Hampshire were angry about the king's control over New Hampshire's land grants and mast trees.

Many New Hampshire colonists had been given land grants to settle the inner parts of the colony. But the king allowed British courts to take the land away from the original settlers and give it to new settlers. This showed how little control colonists had over their lives.

The British navy still used most of New Hampshire's tall pine trees for ship masts. But the colonists needed those trees to build their own homes and ships. They did not want Britain to take the trees.

Colonial Protests

The king finally stopped some of the taxes but not all of them. He kept the tax on tea, glass, and paint. He also continued to fine colonists who cut down pine trees marked with his symbol. Some colonists in Weare refused to pay the fines. Their rebellion was known as the Pine Tree Riot.

Patriots and Loyalists

Many people wanted to break away from Great Britain. They wanted America to have its own government, and they were willing to fight for it. These people were called **Patriots.** They began to talk of a revolution. A *revolution* is a time when people fight to replace one government with a different government.

Other colonists wanted to stay loyal to Britain, and they did not want war. They just wanted the British government to stop demanding taxes and the British soldiers to go back to Britain. These people were called **Loyalists.**

The Boston Massacre

On March 5, 1770, a mob in Boston gathered in front of the customs house, where taxes were paid, to tease a British guard. Then the mob began shouting at the guard and calling him names. He called for help, and British soldiers arrived with their weapons.

The colonists yelled at the soldiers and threw snowballs at them. Suddenly, someone fired a shot. Then more shots rang out. Soon, four colonists were dead and several others were wounded. Another colonist died a few days later. The colonists called the event a massacre. A *massacre* is when lots of people are killed at one time.

The Boston Tea Party

Three years later, a group of men dressed like Indians sneaked on board British tea ships in Boston's harbor. The men dumped the tea into the dark ocean to show the king how angry they were about the tax on tea.

The British leaders were angry, too. They demanded that the colonists pay for the "salt-water tea" and closed Boston Harbor until the colonists did so. Word of the Boston Tea Party spread quickly to the other American colonies.

After the colonists threw the tea overboard, they swept the decks and made sure everything else was in place. They asked a British ship captain to look over the ships and see that no damage was done except to the tea. What do you think the young boys on the shore in this picture were saying to each other?

British Ships in Portsmouth Harbor

When the people of Portsmouth learned about the tea party, the townspeople decided they would not destroy the British tea when it arrived at their port. But they would not allow the tea to be unloaded or sold in their town either.

When a British tea ship docked in Portsmouth Harbor, the people forced it to leave. The ship sailed on—still full of tea—to Canada.

The New Hampshire Colony sent food and supplies to the people in Boston to help them survive until the British reopened Boston Harbor. It was a big step toward uniting the colonies against British rule.

The Colonies Take Action

The 13 colonies knew they had to **cooperate** to solve their problems with Britain. In September 1774, leaders from all the colonies met in Philadelphia, Pennsylvania, at a meeting called the First Continental Congress. **Congress** is a group of representatives who work out problems and make laws.

The Congress demanded that the king end the taxes and open Boston Harbor. The Congress also said the colonists would not trade with Britain or follow its laws until the king agreed to their demands.

What Do You Think ?

Why was it important for the colonies to cooperate with each other as they took a stand against the British?

The members of the Continental Congress discussed many ideas for dealing with the British.

This is how Fort William and Mary looked during colonial days. Do you think the fort looks well protected?

New Castle ●

Fort William and Mary was later renamed Fort Constitution. Today, the site of the attack is on the grounds of the U.S. Coast Guard station in New Castle.

Attack on Fort William and Mary

The cooperation among the colonists worried the king. He knew he had to end the rebellion. He stopped all gunpowder deliveries to the colonies so the people wouldn't be able to use their guns. He also sent his soldiers to take the weapons from the British forts and to threaten the colonists.

When Patriots in Boston heard of the king's plans, Paul Revere rode to Portsmouth. He warned the townspeople that the British would be marching to Fort William and Mary on the island of New Castle. The colonists knew they needed to move the gunpowder before the British soldiers arrived.

Men from Portsmouth and surrounding towns marched to the fort. Only a few British soldiers were guarding it. The colonists fired a few shots, and the British saw they were outnumbered. They quickly *surrendered,* or gave up. No one was killed.

The colonists removed barrels of gunpowder, guns, and bullets, and took down the British flag. The capture of Fort William and Mary was the American colonists' first organized military action against Great Britain.

LESSON ① KEY IDEA REVIEW

1. Name two things King George put a tax on.
2. What did the First Continental Congress demand the king do after the Boston Tea Party occurred?
3. What was the first organized military action the colonists took against Great Britain?

"The British Are Coming!"

By 1775, the king was angry with the rebellious colonists. He sent British troops to Boston to arrest colonial leaders and to take control of military stores of guns and powder. Colonists across New England needed to be warned!

William Dawes, Dr. Samuel Prescott, and Paul Revere mounted their horses and rode all night to warn people about the British soldiers' arrival. At each village and farm they passed, they shouted, "The British are coming!"

When the British soldiers arrived, they marched through Boston. When they reached Lexington, colonists met them with guns. The two sides began shouting at each other. Suddenly, someone fired a gun. Then others began shooting. After the smoke cleared, eight colonists were dead.

The British marched on to Concord, Massachusetts, and met more colonists. The colonists hid behind trees, barns, and stone walls, and fired their guns. The British were not used to that kind of fighting. They fought in a straight line and expected their enemies to do the same. The British *retreated* back to Boston, with the colonists firing on them the entire way.

Key Idea

What was New Hampshire's role in the American Revolution?

Words to Understand

abolish
cause
constitution
declaration
militia
neutral
petition
ratify
regiment
retreat
treason
unalienable

Paul Revere rode through New England, warning the colonists that the British were coming. How would news like this be spread today? Would we ride on horses throughout our towns and cities?

What Do You Think?

Many years later, a poet named Ralph Waldo Emerson called the fighting at Lexington and Concord "the shot heard 'round the world." What do you think he meant?

New Hampshire Enters the Fight

No battles of the American Revolution were fought in New Hampshire. But hundreds of New Hampshire men fought in almost every major battle of the war.

Some battles were fought at sea. The Continental Congress created a navy to keep British ships from bringing more men and supplies to America. New Hampshire shipyards built ships for the navy. One ship was named the *Raleigh*. It is the ship shown on our state seal. The *Raleigh* was the first ship to carry the American flag into battle at sea.

New Hampshire was the only colony in which no battles were fought during the American Revolution.

New Hampshire men served on ships. They attacked British merchant ships. They gave the food and supplies they took from the ships to the colonists. Do you think the men in this picture are fighting on the same side during the American Revolution? Why or why not?

Portsmouth
Exeter

Exeter Becomes the Capital

The king's royal government was located in Portsmouth. When the American Revolution began, some British leaders felt unsafe there and fled. Others remained in Portsmouth throughout the war and stayed loyal to the king. But the colonists did not allow them to have any power.

Many Patriots lived in Exeter, so it became the capital of New Hampshire during the war. It was also the colony's military headquarters.

Battle of Bunker Hill

After the battles of Lexington and Concord, King George sent more soldiers to Boston. Colonists from Massachusetts, Connecticut, and New Hampshire hurried to Boston to fight.

New Hampshire Soldiers

John Stark commanded a New Hampshire regiment. A *regiment* is a large group of soldiers. Most of the soldiers were farmers. They collected the few guns they had from home and left their farms to fight. They arrived in Boston hungry and tired. They were not trained to fight. They didn't have uniforms or sturdy boots. But they did have a *cause*. They were fighting for their freedom and for the freedom of their families.

British Soldiers

The British soldiers wore bright red military uniforms. Their guns were polished. Their cannons were ready for war. They were well-trained fighters and marched in straight rows to their battle positions.

Compare the British soldiers and the colonial militia in this picture. What are some differences between them? What things do they have in common?

What Do You Think ❓

There are many ways to resolve a problem besides fighting. In this case, the colonists felt so strongly about freedom from Great Britain that they risked their lives. Is there a cause important enough to you to consider risking your life for it? What is it?

The British are in the red coats. The colonists are at the top of the hill. From this picture, which side looks like it is winning the battle?

More men from New Hampshire fought in the Battle of Bunker Hill than from Massachusetts and Connecticut combined.

Don't Shoot 'Til You See the Whites of Their Eyes!

John Stark positioned his men so they could keep the British ships from landing their soldiers on the beach of the Mystic River near Breed's Hill.

Stark's plan worked, but the British found another way to get to the hill. Rows and rows of British soldiers climbed up to meet the colonists. The colonists did not have as much gunpowder as the British. They could not waste any of it by firing their guns too soon. Legend says that one leader told the men, "Don't shoot 'til you see the whites of their eyes!"

As soon as the British soldiers were close, the colonists fired their guns. All at once, the hill was full of smoke. Bullets flew everywhere. The British kept coming until they finally captured the hill. Both sides lost many men in the fight, but the British lost more than the colonists. This battle, called the Battle of Bunker Hill, showed the British that the colonists could fight.

Because of John Stark's skill and bravery during the battle, he was made the leader of the entire New Hampshire *militia*.

JOHN STARK
1728–1822

Many people believe New Hampshire's greatest hero of the American Revolution was John Stark. He was known for his bravery in battle and brilliant military leadership. This Patriot was born in Londonderry and later moved to Manchester. When Stark was 24 years old, Indians captured him and took him to the Abenaki village of St. Francis in Canada. He was adopted into the tribe and learned the people's language and customs. Later, the British government paid his ransom, and he returned to New Hampshire. A few years after his capture, Stark was part of Rogers' Rangers during the French and Indian War.

Stark later became a leading American general in the American Revolution. He served under the command of George Washington. He led his soldiers to victory in the Battle of Bennington in Vermont.

Stark married Elizabeth "Molly" Stark. They raised 10 children, five boys and five girls. Molly died when she was 78. John lived to be 94.

A statue of John Stark represents New Hampshire in the U.S. Capitol Building in Washington, D.C. He is the author of our state motto: "Live Free or Die."

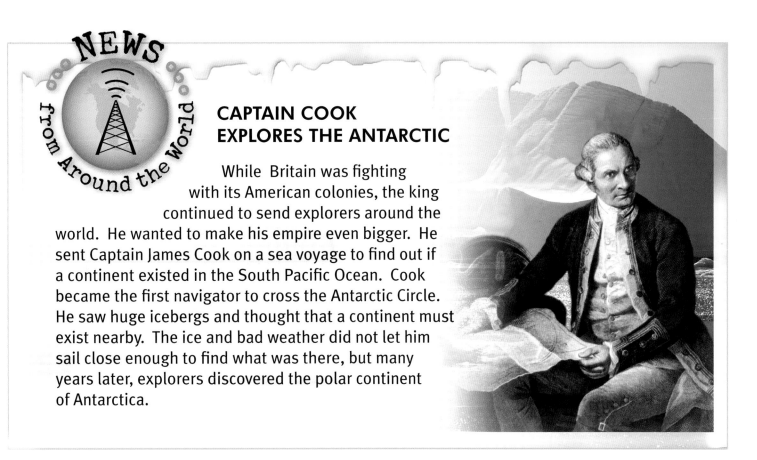

CAPTAIN COOK EXPLORES THE ANTARCTIC

While Britain was fighting with its American colonies, the king continued to send explorers around the world. He wanted to make his empire even bigger. He sent Captain James Cook on a sea voyage to find out if a continent existed in the South Pacific Ocean. Cook became the first navigator to cross the Antarctic Circle. He saw huge icebergs and thought that a continent must exist nearby. The ice and bad weather did not let him sail close enough to find what was there, but many years later, explorers discovered the polar continent of Antarctica.

Life on the Home Front

The war didn't affect only the soldiers who were fighting far away. It also affected the soldiers' families at home. Families struggled to survive without their fathers, sons, and brothers.

Added Work

Life for women became even more difficult than it was before. As always, they had to take care of their young children and do their chores. But with the men at war, women and children also had to take care of the crops. They had to cut down trees and chop wood for fireplaces. They had to hunt animals for food.

Food, clothing, and medicine were scarce during the war. Many families had to depend on their neighbors to survive.

Women had much more work to do with their men away at war. What jobs do you see being done in this picture?

PATRIOT OR LOYALIST?

People used art as a way to express how they felt about the Revolution and to show which side of the war they supported. Tavern owners painted their signs to tell visitors if they were Loyalists or Patriots. New Hampshire soldiers carried flags into battles during the war. They decorated their flags to identify their regiments.

Look at these regiment flags and symbols used to decorate them. Why do you think these symbols were chosen? What do you think the symbols stand for? If you created your own flag, what kinds of symbols would you use?

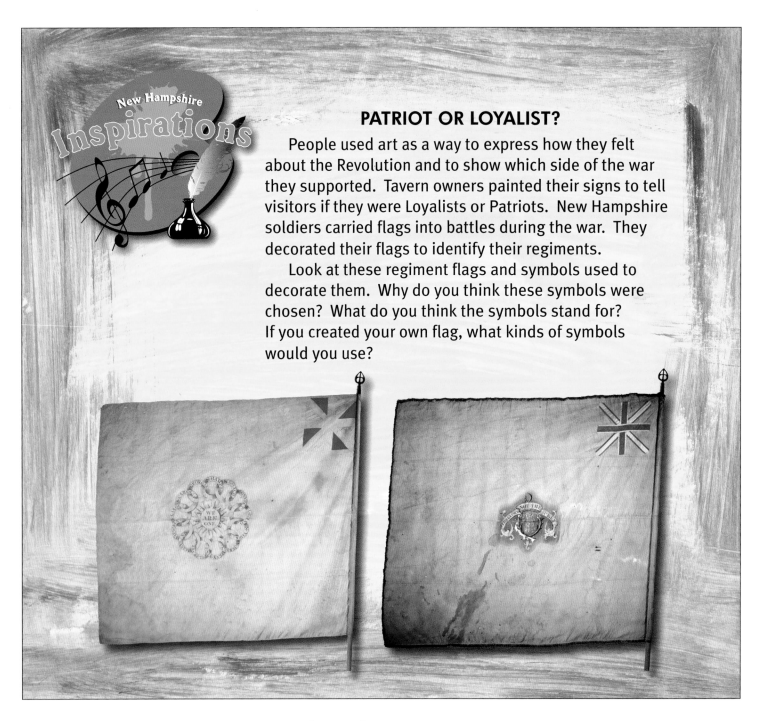

Role of Native Americans

The war affected the lives of Native Americans, too. Some tried to remain *neutral* during the war and refused to join the fighting. Others fought for the American side or the British side. Can you think of reasons a Native American might have chosen to fight for the colonists? Can you think of reasons he might have fought for the British?

Preparing for a New Government

Do you remember Governor John Wentworth? He was the royal governor of the colony for many years. When the Revolution started, Wentworth remained loyal to Britain. Fearing for his safety, he left Portsmouth. After he left, New Hampshire's revolutionary leaders wrote a new constitution in January 1776. A *constitution* describes how a government is organized. New Hampshire was the first colony to write a constitution and form a government separate from Britain.

The constitution was written quickly, so New Hampshire would have some kind of government during the war. It stated that an elected assembly of men would govern the colony. There would be no governor.

The Western Rebellion

Not everyone liked the new constitution. Settlers living in the western part of the colony had not helped create it. They felt their needs and opinions had been ignored, so they refused to pay any taxes outlined in the constitution. They threatened to form their own government or join Vermont. These are the things they did not like about the constitution:

- They did not feel they had enough representation in the new government.
- They did not believe the rights of New Hampshire's people were secure.
- They wanted the power to *ratify* (approve) the constitution.
- They thought the capital in Exeter was too far away from western towns. They wanted the capital moved to a more central location.

The settlers' concerns led to the rewriting of the constitution in 1784, after the Revolution. The new document allowed each town to be represented in state government, permitted the legislature to hold meetings in different locations around the state, and gave people the right to ratify and make changes to the constitution. Although some things have been added to it, the second constitution still governs our state today.

A

CONSTITUTION,

CONTAINING A

BILL of RIGHTS,

AND

FORM of GOVERNMENT,

Agreed upon by the DELEGATES

OF THE

PEOPLE of the State of NEW-HAMPSHIRE,

IN

CONVENTION,

Held at CONCORD, on the firſt Tueſday of *June* 1783; ſubmitted to, and approved of by the People of ſaid State; and eſtabliſhed by their Delegates in Convention, *October* 31, 1783.

PRINTED AT PORTSMOUTH, IN THE STATE OF NEW-HAMPSHIRE, 1783.

This is the New Hampshire constitution. Where was the convention for the constitution held? When and where was it printed?

These are the freedom papers for Amos Fortune dated December 30, 1763.

A Petition for Freedom

Not everyone in the colony enjoyed the freedoms and rights described in the new constitution. When the Revolution began, there were more than 600 slaves in the colony. A few **petitioned** New Hampshire's new government for the abolition of slavery. **Abolish** means to do away with something. But the leaders refused to discuss the petition.

Many slaves earned their freedom in exchange for serving in the military during the Revolution. Others were freed by their masters after the war ended. By 1790, there were only 158 slaves in New Hampshire. Ten years later, there were only eight.

NEW HAMPSHIRE PORTRAIT

This compass belonged to Amos Fortune.

AMOS FORTUNE
1710–1801

Amos Fortune was born in Africa and taken to America as a slave. His master was Ichabod Richardson, a tanner in Massachusetts. Richardson taught Amos the tanning trade. It was hard, smelly work, but he was good at it.

Fortune earned money from tanning hides. He saved his money and bought his freedom when he was 60 years old.

Fortune wanted to make a good life for himself. He bought some land and built a house. He soon fell in love with a slave named Lydia Somerset. Fortune paid for her freedom, and they were married. Sadly, she died just three months later. The next year, Fortune met another slave named Violate. He purchased her freedom, and they were married the next day.

Fortune and Violate left Massachusetts when Amos was 71 years old. They settled in Jaffrey and adopted a daughter named Celyndia. Fortune built a home and a tannery in Jaffrey. His tannery business was very successful. He used some of the money to help start the Jaffrey Social Library.

When Fortune died, he was a respected and wealthy member of the Jaffrey community. He left most of his wealth to his family and made a donation to the church. The rest of his money was given to the town of Jaffrey to support the local school.

The Declaration of Independence

New Hampshire was the first colony to officially declare its independence from Great Britain. After New Hampshire wrote its constitution, the colony sent delegates to meet with the Second Continental Congress, which had been organized in Philadelphia in May 1775.

At this meeting, the members agreed that all the colonies would break away from Britain and start a new country. Thomas Jefferson of Virginia wrote a statement to the entire world to announce the decision. He called the statement the Declaration of Independence. A *declaration* is an announcement that tells people about an important decision.

After it was written, copies of the Declaration were read aloud to people in all the colonies. After hearing its words, leaders declared New Hampshire a state.

Tanners tanned skins of very young calves to make parchment, a smooth writing paper. The Declaration of Independence and the U.S. Constitution were both written on this special parchment.

These men are writing the Declaration of Independence. What clue in the picture tells you the men went through many drafts?

What Does the Declaration Say?

On July 4, 1776, the Continental Congress approved the Declaration of Independence. It explained why the colonists went to war against Britain:

- The colonists had rights that could not be taken away. They believed "all men are created equal, that they are endowed by their Creator with certain *unalienable* Rights, that among these are Life, Liberty, and the pursuit of Happiness."

- A government should protect these rights.

- If the government did not protect those rights, then people could start a new government.

- Governments get their power from the people.

- The British government and king had hurt the colonists in many ways.

The Signers Risked It All

Although the Declaration was approved in July, it was not signed until August. When John Hancock of Massachusetts signed it, he wrote his name large enough for King George to read it without his glasses.

Most of the signers were wealthy men. They were respected in their towns. For the sake of liberty, they risked everything they had, and they knew it. To sign the Declaration of Independence was an act of **treason**, or going against the government. The punishment for treason was death. Three of these brave signers were from New Hampshire.

By signing the Declaration, the leaders knew the states were on their way to becoming a new country. But it was not going to be easy. The American Revolution lasted several more years.

1729–1795

Dr. Josiah Bartlett was born in Massachusetts. He studied medicine as a young man and moved to Kingston to open his medical practice. Dr. Bartlett represented New Hampshire at the Second Continental Congress and was the second person to sign the Declaration. He served as chief justice of the New Hampshire Supreme Court. He was also New Hampshire's first acting state governor.

"And for the support of this Declaration . . . we mutually pledge to each other our Lives, our Fortunes and our sacred Honor."

—Final words of the Declaration of Independence

Matthew Thornton was born in Northern Ireland and came to America when he was very young. As a young man, Matthew worked as a doctor in Londonderry. He later moved to Merrimack and lived in a place known today as Thornton's Ferry. Governor Benning Wentworth granted him land near the White Mountains, and today this town is known as Thornton.

Thornton was 61 when the American Revolution began, so he did not fight in the war. Instead, Dr. Thornton held positions in the court and other offices. He was not in Philadelphia when the Declaration of Independence was ready to be signed. He was one of the last men to sign it later that year.

1714–1803

William Whipple was born in Maine. He was the son of a sea captain and became a sailor himself. William became captain of his own ship when he was only 21. He commanded trading voyages to the West Indies and Europe. After he retired from life at sea, Captain Whipple became a businessman in Portsmouth. At the start of the American Revolution, he devoted his life to politics. Whipple was the third signer of the Declaration of Independence.

1730–1785

LESSON 2 KEY IDEA REVIEW

1. Why was war hard for women who stayed home and for the men who went to fight?
2. What are the main points of the Declaration of Independence?
3. Why was it considered a major risk to sign the Declaration of Independence?

Key Idea

What did the leaders of the new country of the United States want in their new government?

Words to Understand

amend
amendment
branch
executive
judicial
legislative

New Hampshire's delegates to the Constitutional Convention were John Langdon and Nicholas Gilman. George Washington is standing at the front of the room.

Ending the War

The last major battle of the American Revolution took place five years after the signing of the Declaration of Independence. Thousands of British soldiers surrendered to the colonists after the bloody Battle of Yorktown in Virginia. For the next two years, the Americans and the British held meetings to find ways to peacefully end the war. Finally, leaders on both sides signed a document called the Treaty of Paris. In the treaty, Great Britain accepted the independence of the United States of America.

National Government for the People

With the war over, the states could begin building a new nation. The states sent delegates to a meeting in Philadelphia to discuss new laws and ideas for the country. The meeting was called the Constitutional Convention.

The delegates created the Constitution of the United States. It divided the U.S. government into three *branches: executive, legislative,* and *judicial*. These branches would work together to govern the country. We still use the three branches in our government today.

Constitution of the United States

The U.S. government is based on our Constitution. Here are some of its main points:

- The people run the government. We vote for who we want to represent us. We vote for who we want to lead us.
- The Constitution is the highest law of the land.
- Power is divided among the president, Congress, and the courts.
- The people can change, or **amend,** the Constitution.
- There will be an army to defend America in case of war.
- The president will lead the army.

Delegates from each state signed the Constitution when its wording was complete. The delegates agreed that at least nine states would have to ratify the Constitution before it could go into effect. In June 1788, New Hampshire became the ninth state to ratify it.

What Do You Think?

What are the first three words of the Constitution? Why do you think a government run by the people was so important to the creators of the Constitution?

The Bill of Rights

Many people believed the new Constitution did not protect the rights of the people. They wanted a document that listed basic rights for each citizen. A few years after the Constitution was signed, 10 *amendments* were added to it. The first 10 amendments to the Constitution are called the Bill of Rights.

1ST AMENDMENT

Freedom of religion: You can worship as you wish or not at all. The government cannot choose one religion for the whole country.

Freedom of speech: As long as your words do not cause danger or harm to other people, you can express your opinion about any subject without being arrested. You can even say things against the government.

Freedom of press: The government cannot tell people what they can and cannot print in newspapers or books.

Freedom of assembly: You can join and meet with any group.

2ND AMENDMENT

Right to bear arms: Adults can own guns for legal activities.

3RD AMENDMENT

Right to not have soldiers in your home during peacetime: In the past, kings made people feed and house soldiers not only during wars but also in times of peace.

4TH AMENDMENT

Freedom from improper search and seizure: You have a right to privacy. If police believe you have something illegal in your home or car, they have to get a search warrant before searching your things.

5TH, 6TH, AND 7TH AMENDMENTS

These protect you if you are accused of a crime. They include the right to a speedy trial and a trial by jury.

8TH AMENDMENT

The government is not allowed to punish you in a cruel and unusual way.

9TH AMENDMENT

People can have other rights not named in the Bill of Rights.

10TH AMENDMENT

The national government does not have all the power in the United States. State governments have a lot of power, too.

What Do You Think ?

The Constitution and the Bill of Rights define many rights that our government guarantees to citizens of the United States. Why is it important to have these rights listed?

LESSON ③ KEY IDEA REVIEW

1. What three branches of government did the Constitutional Convention create?
2. What is the highest law of the land?
3. What is the Bill of Rights?

Go to the Source

An Engraving
of the Boston Massacre

This is an engraving of the Boston Massacre by Paul Revere. The title is "The bloody massacre perpetrated in King Street Boston on March 5th 1770 by a party of the 29th Regt."

LOOK

Why is "The bloody massacre" a good title for the picture?

THINK

What other ways do you think these people could solve their conflict?

DECIDE

How does the engraving help us to learn about history?

Chapter 6

Spotlighting Geography   The Location of the Capital

When the site for Washington, D.C., was chosen over 200 years ago, it was in the center of the 13 states. Today, it is not in the middle of all of the states. Use the map of the United States in the atlas on page 270 to answer the questions.

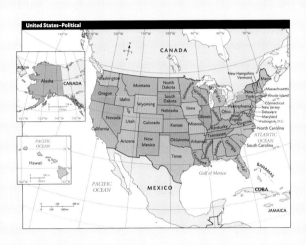

United States–Political

1. About how many states would a government leader from California have to cross to get to Washington, D.C.?
2. If a government leader from Concord had a meeting in Washington, D.C., about how many miles would he or she have to travel?
3. If you could choose a new location for our nation's capital, where would it be? Why would you choose that location?

Becoming a Better Reader   Find the Main Idea

When reading nonfiction information, good readers always keep in mind the main idea of what they are reading. Thinking about the main idea helps good readers organize the new information they gather as they read. Main ideas can be found in chapter and lesson titles and in headings. What is the main idea of this chapter? What was life like during the American Revolution? Write a paragraph stating the main idea and three supporting ideas using the titles of the chapter and lessons to help you.

Reviewing the Big Idea

1. Describe what happened during the Revolutionary War.
2. Paraphrase the Declaration of Independence.
3. How does the Bill of Rights affect your daily life?
4. Contrast the British monarchy and the new government formed after the war.
5. Develop a list of reasons for why the British and the colonists were fighting the American Revolution.
6. Who had a stronger cause? Why?

A New State in a New Nation

Big Idea

What challenges did New Hampshire and the United States face as they grew?

New industries began to grow in New Hampshire during this time. So did towns and cities. This is a painting of Manchester. What industry do you see in the picture?

Timeline of Events

1803
The Louisiana Purchase

1808
The state capital is relocated to Concord.

1800

1810

1809–1810
Mill construction begins along the Merrimack River in Manchester.

1812–1815
War of 1812

The years following the American Revolution brought important changes to New Hampshire and the United States. Leaders struggled to build state and national governments. New forms of transportation and communication were invented. New job opportunities changed the ways Americans worked and lived.

1820s
Farm girls begin working in mills.

1827
The first Concord coach is built.

1832
The Republic of Indian Stream is organized.

1850s
Immigrants begin replacing farm girls in mills.

1820	1830	1840	1850

1816
Construction of the State House in Concord begins.

1838
Amoskeag Manufacturing Company designs the layout for the city of Manchester.

153

What changes took place after the American Revolution?

Words to Understand

agriculture
cargo
economy
frontier
inspect
invention

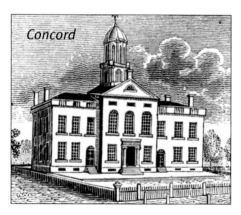
Concord

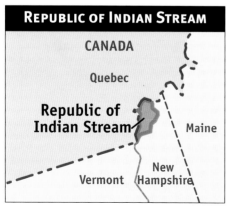
REPUBLIC OF INDIAN STREAM

CANADA

Quebec

Republic of Indian Stream

Maine

Vermont

New Hampshire

Life after the Revolution

Americans won their independence from Great Britain. They no longer lived under a government ruled by kings and queens. But freedom brought many challenges to leaders of the new country. They had to create a national government. Each state also had to build its government.

Building a State Government

When the American Revolution ended, New Hampshire leaders worked to better organize the state's government. As they did this, two major issues came up:

- Where would the state capital be located?
- Where would New Hampshire's northern border with Canada be located?

Concord ★

Revolutionary leaders had relocated the state capital to Exeter during the war. But many residents complained that Exeter was too far away from people in some areas of the state. Lawmakers agreed to meet in Concord instead.

Another question state leaders had to answer was the location of the borders between the United States and Canada.

The United States and British-ruled Canada both claimed the land around Indian Stream. Both countries issued land grants to settlers there and demanded taxes from the residents.

The 300 people living in Indian Stream Territory did not want to belong to either country. Instead, they formed their own country. The citizens of the Republic of Indian Stream wrote a constitution, elected leaders, created courts, formed a militia, and even printed their own money and postage stamps.

The Republic existed until the British gave up their claim four years later. Daniel Webster helped define the border between New Hampshire and Canada. The Republic agreed to become part of New Hampshire. It was later renamed Pittsburg.

JOHN LANGDON
1741–1819

One of New Hampshire's most well-known state leaders was John Langdon. Many people know him because he had the honor of swearing President George Washington into office.

John was born on a farm in Portsmouth. He became a sea captain when he was 22 years old and sailed trading voyages across the Atlantic Ocean. After many years, John returned to Portsmouth and became a shipbuilder.

At the start of the American Revolution, John led 400 other colonists in the attack on the British Fort William and Mary. During the war, John also helped build warships at his shipyard in Portsmouth.

John was a representative at the Second Continental Congress and the Constitutional Convention. He later served in our state's legislature and as governor.

You can visit John's home. It is very fancy and was often the scene of grand parties in John's day. One famous visitor to the house was George Washington.

DANIEL WEBSTER
1782–1852

Daniel Webster was born in a log cabin in Salisbury. His family was very poor, but his parents believed in education. They sent Daniel to Phillips Exeter Academy and later to Dartmouth College. Daniel is called "Dartmouth's Favorite Son."

As a young man, Daniel was terrified of public speaking. But in college, he learned to become an excellent public speaker. He served in many positions in the U.S. government. He created the Webster-Ashburton Treaty that defined the United States border with Canada and improved relations with England.

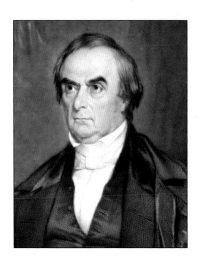

Daniel died after he fell off his horse and suffered a head injury. There are many things and places in our state named for Daniel.

A New Nation, New Problems

While New Hampshire's leaders worked to establish state government, national leaders were trying to build relationships between the United States and other countries. Americans wanted to sell timber and furs to other countries. They wanted to buy things they could not grow themselves, such as tea and sugar. Shipping goods in and out of American ports was important to the new country's *economy*.

War of 1812

But something was keeping America from trading with other countries—a war between Great Britain and France. Their fight caused many problems for American ships.

The British navy stopped American ships at sea and *inspected* their *cargo*. The British also forced American sea captains to pay money to cross the ocean and kept American ships from delivering products to France. The British navy boarded American ships. They captured the seamen and forced them to work on British ships.

These are U.S. soldiers and sailors who fought in the War of 1812. How do they look different from the colonial soldiers described in chapter 6?

156

This angered Americans, so they declared war on Britain in 1812. Although no battles were fought in New Hampshire, our state sent thousands of men to join the fight taking place on the Atlantic Ocean and in other states.

When the war ended years later, both countries claimed to be the winner. However, the war had two important results for the United States: first, Britain stopped capturing American sailors and demanding fees from American ships; second, the Native American tribes east of the Mississippi River that had helped the British were defeated. With less fear of Indian attacks, many Americans were encouraged to move west.

This is a painting of the Battle of Lake Erie, the most important naval battle in the War of 1812. Study the painting closely. What do you think happened right before this scene?

Families couldn't bring much with them on their journeys west. They had to live off the land. What things in this picture did this family get from the land?

The Louisiana Territory

Go West!

In 1803, the United States purchased a large amount of land from France. The Louisiana Purchase, as the land was known, more than doubled the size of the United States. President Jefferson bought the land for only $0.03 an acre!

After the War of 1812, merchants, farmers, and ranchers headed west from East Coast towns to settle on the new land in the hopes of making better lives for themselves. Journeys over mountains and across prairies were always difficult and often dangerous. Some people walked the entire way to the western *frontier*. Others rode on horseback or in wagons.

NEW HAMPSHIRE PORTRAIT

HORACE GREELEY
1811–1872

Horace Greeley was a newspaper editor who encouraged people to move west. He is known for the phrase "Go West, Young Man," but the words were actually written by a reporter in Indiana.

Horace was born in Amherst in a small, one-story farmhouse. His family was poor and worked hard to survive.

Horace's mother taught him to read with a book in her lap while he sat on the floor. "I soon [learned to read] from a book sidewise or upside down . . . which became a subject of neighborhood wonder," he said.

He married Mary Young Cheney and had seven children. Only two survived to adulthood. Horace moved his family to New York City and started the *New York Tribune* newspaper.

Horace used his newspaper to argue for the peaceful end of slavery in the United States. He supported Abraham Lincoln in his run for president of the United States.

Farming in New Hampshire

Not everyone in New Hampshire headed west. Most people stayed on their family farms.

Since colonial times, New Hampshire's families had relied on *agriculture* to make a living. Farming was still important in the 19th century, too. New inventions made farming easier and allowed some families to produce more crops than they could use themselves. The families sold these extra crops to earn money. Railroads made it possible to transport farm products from one town or state to another.

County fairs still mark the arrival of harvest season. The Deerfield Fair is one of the oldest fairs in New England. For more than 130 years, farmers have been bringing their best livestock and crops to the fair to compete for prizes.

Nineteenth-Century Farming Inventions

An *invention* is a new product, service, or idea created by someone. Many inventions changed the way farmers worked:

- The cast-iron tip plough replaced the wooden-tipped plough. This made farming rocky soils of New England easier.

- The reaping machine replaced the scythe. Farmers could cut grain faster than ever before.

- When the threshing machine was invented, farmers no longer had to separate the grain from the rest of the plant by hand.

- Barbed wire helped farmers keep their cattle from roaming off.

This is an ad for farming machines. Do you recognize any of the machines? Do you think farmers still use those same machines today?

As people moved farther west into new territories, new inventions helped them start big farms on the wide, open lands. The westward migration changed New Hampshire farming. Small, rocky New England farms could not easily compete with the large western farms.

Family Farms

Taking care of the family farm was a big job, and everyone had to help—even the small children. Read about the family farm, and imagine all the work you would have to do each day if you were a farmer.

Farmhouse

This was where the family lived and where women did most of their work. Relatives, laborers, and even passing travelers often lived on the farm, so there wasn't much privacy!

Barn

This was used to store hay to feed cattle, horses, and sheep over the winter. Tools such as plows, shovels, and axes were also stored there. Some animals were also kept in the barn at night.

Corn Crib

This is where the family stored corn after it was harvested and shucked. This building allowed air in and out so that the corn would stay fresh.

Smokehouse

This was a small building with a dirt floor. Farmers used hickory bark and corncobs to fuel a fire inside. They hung meats above the fire. The smoke from the fire preserved the meat, or kept it from spoiling.

Root Cellar

This was where families stored vegetables to keep them cold. It also kept vegetables from freezing during winters. It was built partly underground.

Workshop

Although farming was the family's main business, a workshop was where the farmers operated other businesses during times when they were not farming. These businesses helped to pay for other things their families needed. Farmers built workshops for carpentry, blacksmithing, cabinetmaking, coopering, shoemaking, spinning, tanning, weaving, or woodworking.

Woodshed

The family stored chopped wood here. The woodshed helped to keep wood dry and protected from rain and snow. What kinds of things do you think they used the wood for?

Carriage House

This house protected wagons and carriages from bad weather. On some family farms, a small stable was sometimes included in the carriage house. Animals could stay in the stable at night.

Outhouse

During this time period, homes did not have bathrooms inside of them. The outhouse was a small building where one or more toilets were located. Can you imagine what it would be like to use an outhouse instead of the bathroom in your house?

Chicken Coop

This was a pen where chickens were kept and fed. The family could collect fresh eggs from here daily.

School Rules

Besides working on their family farms, many children also went to school for eight weeks in the summer and eight weeks in the winter. Just like today, students had to follow many school rules. But so did teachers! Look at the rules teachers had to follow in the 1800s.

1. Teacher will fill lamps, trim wicks, and clean chimneys.
2. Each morning teacher will bring bucket of water and a scuttle of coal for the day's session.
3. Make your pens carefully. You may whittle nibs to the individual taste of the pupils.
4. Men teachers may take one evening each week for courting purposes or two evenings a week if they attend church regularly.
5. After 10 hours in school, the teachers may spend the remaining time reading the Bible or any other good book.
6. Women teachers who marry or engage in unseemly conduct will be dismissed.
7. Every teacher should lay aside for each payday a goodly sum of his earning for his benefit during his declining years so that he will not become a burden on society.
8. Any teacher who smokes, uses liquor in any form, frequents pool or public halls, or gets shaved in a barber shop will give good reason to suspect his worth, intention, integrity, and honesty.

Activity — Teaching Then and Now

Reread the eight school rules. With a partner, discuss people's values in the 1800s. What kind of character did teachers have to have?

Now identify which rules above apply to today's teachers. For each rule that doesn't apply, write a sentence about why it doesn't. How are our values today different from those of the 1800s?

LESSON 1 KEY IDEA REVIEW

1. Where was the new state capital located?
2. How was the Indian Stream border decided?
3. Why did many people move west?

Better Transportation

As the 1800s progressed, the new nation became stronger, and many changes began to take place. New inventions and changes helped our country and our state become connected to other places. One of the most important changes occurred in *transportation*. New ways of moving people and products from one place to another allowed towns to grow, businesses to expand, and wilderness areas to be explored.

Covered Bridges

Covered bridges are beautiful symbols of New Hampshire's past. As the state's population increased, so did its need for new roads. Workers built bridges over the state's many rivers and streams to connect new roads. Wooden bridges were very slippery in the rain and snow, so workers added roofs and siding to them. This also protected the bridges from being worn by the weather.

There are still over 50 covered bridges on New Hampshire's back roads. The oldest one, built in 1829, is the Bath-Haverhill Bridge.

Key Idea

What improvements in transportation and communication helped connect people and places in the 19th century?

Words to Understand

cable
coach
cog
communication
framework
transportation

This is the Flume Covered Bridge on the Pemigewasset River. Covered bridges such as this helped travelers to safely cross rivers during bad weather. Have you seen any of these bridges around our state?

These horses are pulling a wooden snow roller over a snow-covered road so that wagons can use the road. Do you think this looks like a good way to clear the path?

Snow Rollers

Roads were not paved at this time. They were made of dirt or stones. When heavy snow fell, the roads had to be rolled flat so wagons and sleighs could travel over them. Horses pulled big snow rollers over roads to open up pathways.

Expansion of the Railroads

By the middle of the 1800s, railroad tracks stretched across New Hampshire and connected the state to the rest of the country. Merchants could ship their goods in and out of the state. Workers could leave farms and small towns, and travel to larger cities to work in factories and mills.

What Do You Think ?

During the 1800s, people traveled by foot, horseback, or in wagons. How many ways do people travel today?

This picture shows a locomotive made by the Amoskeag Manufacturing Company. A locomotive is an engine that helps to pull or push a train. Prior to the Civil War, Amoskeag machine shops made over 200 of these.

A climber named Sylvester Marsh got caught in a storm while climbing Mount Washington in 1857. He survived the long night on the mountain. But the experience inspired him to build a railway to the top so others could visit it easily and safely.

The Mount Washington Cog Railway was completed in July 1869. It was named "Old Peppersass." Coal-fired and smoke-spewing, it was the first *cog* railway built to the top of any mountain in the world. The Cog was the most advanced railway project of its day.

Today's Cog Railway uses 1,000 gallons of water and burns a ton of coal on each trip up and down the mountain. Have you ever taken a ride on this famous train?

Concord Coach

J. Stephen Abbott and Lewis Downing of Concord were carriage and wheel makers. They hated traveling in uncomfortable wagons or carriages made with metal springs. The springs bounced travelers up and down as they rode over bumpy roads. Abbot and Downing created a *coach* that made travel smoother and more comfortable.

Concord coaches were built on *frameworks* with folded leather straps that formed strong supports underneath the sitting areas. Passengers did not have to bounce up and down inside the coach anymore. Many people rode in Concord coaches on their journeys to the western frontier.

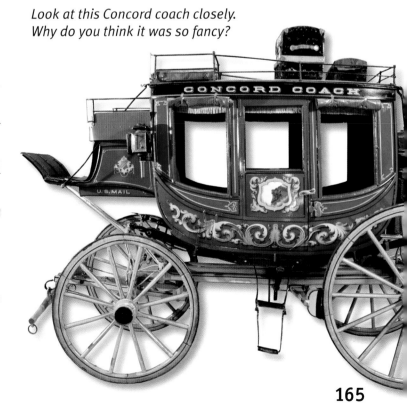

Look at this Concord coach closely. Why do you think it was so fancy?

Better Communication

As families moved west, they needed ways to keep in touch with their families back east, so people began to improve *communication*.

Newspapers

During colonial times, the *New Hampshire Gazette* was the only major newspaper in New Hampshire. Following the Revolution, more than a dozen newspapers were started. One was even published on top of Mount Washington!

Among the Clouds

In the late 1800s, Mount Washington became a popular tourist site. Visitors from all over New England spent summer months enjoying the natural beauty of the mountain from on top of its peak in a beautiful hotel. To keep mountain guests and nearby valley communities updated about local and national news, *Among the Clouds* was published daily in the summer. It was the nation's first newspaper printed on top of a mountain.

The New Hampshire Gazette's *editors claim the newspaper is the oldest in the nation.*

This is a copy of Among the Clouds. *What is special about this newspaper?*

Telegraph

In colonial times, the fastest way to send messages back and forth was on horseback. The invention of the telegraph, however, made communicating faster and much easier. The telegraph used wires and electricity to send and receive messages over long distances.

Transatlantic Cable

If people wanted to communicate with others across the Atlantic Ocean, they had to send letters on ships. It took months for letters to get back and forth. Imagine waiting that long to send and receive e-mails!

To make communication across the ocean easier, workers sunk a giant telegraph *cable* into the water. The cable ran all the way from Ireland to Rye Beach. It was over 3,000 miles long!

Linking the Present to the Past

How do you talk to your friends today? What ways can you communicate with your friends that were not invented when your parents or grandparents were your age?

These workers are trying to sink part of the Transatlantic Cable into the ocean. Look carefully at the picture. What has happened to the cable?

LESSON 2 KEY IDEA REVIEW

1. What is the Cog Railway?
2. What was the name of the first newspaper printed on a mountaintop?
3. What was the telegraph?

Key Idea

How did the rise of mills in New Hampshire affect people's lives?

Words to Understand

condition
famine
illegal
manufacture
product
situation
textile

The Rise of Industry

A revolution occurred in England in the 18th century and spread to the United States. It was called the Industrial Revolution, but it was not a war.

The Industrial Revolution changed the way things were made in our country. It changed the way people worked. Instead of families making their own shoes and clothing items at home, factories and mills used machines to *manufacture* thousands of goods at once. The *products* were sold to families all over the world. Items made in the mills were created faster, cheaper, and usually better than ever before.

Textile Mills

New Hampshire's many rivers were good for powering mills. One of New Hampshire's most important mill products was *textiles*. For the first time in American history, the process of turning cotton into fabric was done in one location and on a large scale. Mills made yards and yards of brightly colored fabrics and sold them around the world.

STEP 1: ARRIVAL

Trains delivered large bales of matted cotton (or wool) to factories. Workers put the cotton into machines that fluffed it into tufts. Then they put the cotton tufts on a moving belt that took them to a picker room.

168

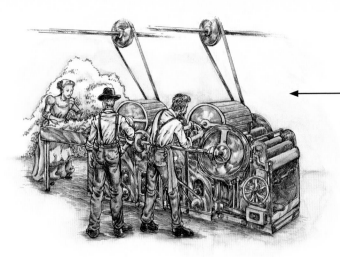

STEP 2: PICKING

Early mill workers removed dirt, insects, leaves, and seeds from the cotton by hand, but later, picking machines sped up the process. The machines' rotating teeth removed the waste and pressed the cotton into sheets called laps.

STEP 3: CARDING

Workers fed each lap into a carding machine that pulled the fibers over rotating tubes. The tubes had wire teeth that further cleaned the cotton. Next, machines twisted the cotton into thin, loose strands called slivers. Slivers were combined and twisted into threads.

STEP 4: SPINNING

Spinning machines called throttles and spinning mules twisted the thin threads and wound them into yarn on bobbins.

STEP 5: WARPING

Warping machines combined the yarns from several bobbins and wound them close together on a spool.

STEP 6: WEAVING

Workers ran powerful looms that wove the yarn into cloth.

STEP 7: FINISHED CLOTH

Workers inspected the cloth and, if needed, repaired it. They bleached some cloth and dyed the other cloths different colors and patterns.

A New State in a New Nation

Amoskeag Manufacturing Company

Amoskeag Manufacturing Company was the most powerful company in New Hampshire for nearly 100 years. At its peak, it was the largest textile manufacturer in the world. It had more than 17,000 workers.

When Amoskeag first opened on the Merrimack River, most of its workers came from local towns and farms. Later, workers came from France, Canada, Ireland, Poland, Scotland, and Germany.

The company created an entire city for its workers. It built houses, provided child care, created parks and streets, and donated land for churches and cemeteries.

By the mid-1800s, Amoskeag was known for its fine textiles. As years passed, the company also made shoes, sewing machines, guns, and trains.

Although the Amoskeag Manufacturing Company no longer exists, its mills in Manchester are still an important part of the city. Many new businesses use the mile-long stretch of brick mill buildings that line the Merrimack River. Restaurants, a radio station, and a museum have all been named for the mills. City streets are named after people and things that relate to mill history.

These girls worked in a New Hampshire mill. Would you be willing to work to help your family survive?

Mill Girls

Mills created new jobs for New Hampshire's people. Farming was a difficult way to earn a living because it depended on things like weather and seasons. Mills operated in all kinds of weather all year long. Workers earned a paycheck every month and could use their wages to buy food and clothing.

The first mill workers were mostly young, unmarried farm girls. Mill work gave them money to send home to help their families survive. It also gave the girls a chance to escape farm life for a while.

The girls lived in boarding houses owned by the mill company. Four girls usually shared one room. They were required to attend church and to follow strict rules of behavior set by the mill owners.

Struggles in the Mills

As the mill companies grew, mill owners expected the girls to work up to 12 hours each day, six days a week. They did not pay the girls more money for the longer work hours.

The work was difficult, dirty, and dangerous. The sound of hundreds of machines running at one time was deafening. Air in workrooms was filled with tiny fibers of cotton and dust. Many girls injured their hands in fast-moving equipment and caught their long hair in looms.

Mill girls became angry about the long hours and dangerous **conditions**. They did not dare complain to their bosses because they feared losing their jobs. Instead, many wrote letters to local newspapers about their **situation:**

Women mill workers at Cocheco Mills (shown here) in Dover were the first to protest conditions in the mills by refusing to work until their situation improved.

What are we coming to? Here am I, a healthy New England Girl, quite well-behaved bestowing . . . half of all my hours including Sundays, upon a company, for less than two cents an hour. . . .

—Octavia

You don't realize how unpleasant it is . . . to be confined in a factory month after month, with no time to enjoy the sunshine and flowers, the blue sky and the green grass.

—A factory girl

A Changing Workforce

Mills needed workers as badly as workers needed jobs. But something happened in the mid-1800s that sent thousands of new workers to the mills and allowed owners to ignore mill girls' requests for better wages and working conditions.

Life in Europe and Canada was more difficult than in the United States. Thousands of immigrants came to the United States hoping to find jobs in mills and factories.

The immigrants wanted to start their new lives in America. They agreed to work in the low-paying mills so they could take care of their families. Most of the mill girls returned home to their farms or found other ways to earn money.

"Why did our people leave Canada and come to the States? Because they had to make sure of a living for their family and themselves. . . . The wages paid by the textile mills was the attraction."

—Philippe Lemay, French Canadian textile worker

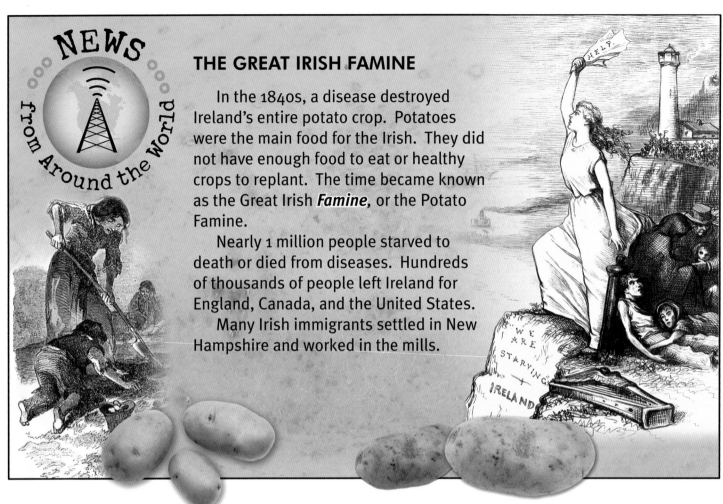

THE GREAT IRISH FAMINE

In the 1840s, a disease destroyed Ireland's entire potato crop. Potatoes were the main food for the Irish. They did not have enough food to eat or healthy crops to replant. The time became known as the Great Irish *Famine,* or the Potato Famine.

Nearly 1 million people starved to death or died from diseases. Hundreds of thousands of people left Ireland for England, Canada, and the United States.

Many Irish immigrants settled in New Hampshire and worked in the mills.

Children in the Mills

Parents often did not earn enough money in the mills to care for their families, so many immigrant children quit school to work in the mills. Their paychecks helped their families survive.

In the 1870s, leaders passed a law that made it *illegal* for a child under 12 to work in the mills unless he or she had completed school the year before. Children and parents often lied about children's ages so they could get jobs.

Many years later, a photographer named Lewis Wickes Hine became famous for his photographs of immigrant families. Many of his photos show children working in factories during the Industrial Revolution. The pictures were shown in national magazines and on posters. People who did not live in industrial cities were very upset about the way children were being treated in factories. Many believed children should not be allowed to do the dirty, dangerous work.

These boys worked long hours in a mill. Would you like to work every day instead of going to school?

INCREDIBLE INVENTIONS

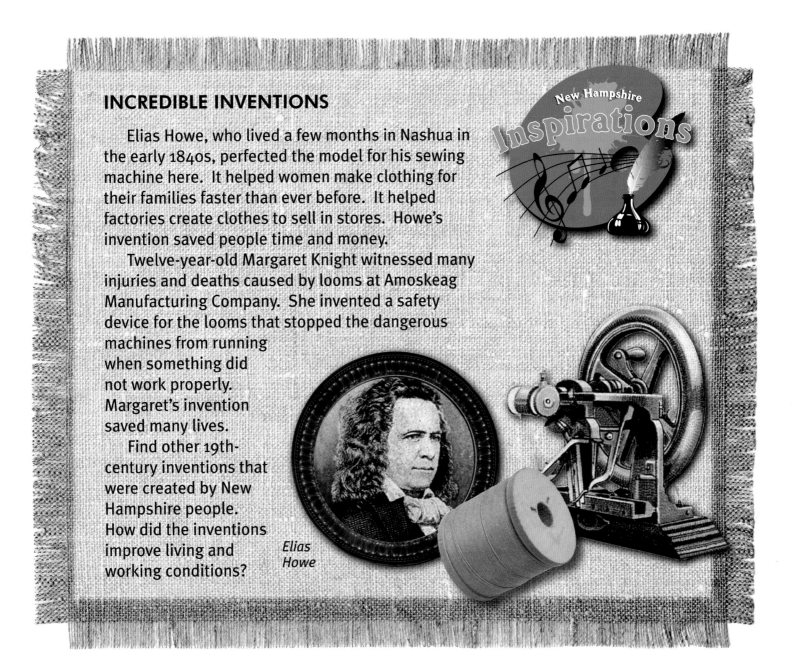

Elias Howe, who lived a few months in Nashua in the early 1840s, perfected the model for his sewing machine here. It helped women make clothing for their families faster than ever before. It helped factories create clothes to sell in stores. Howe's invention saved people time and money.

Twelve-year-old Margaret Knight witnessed many injuries and deaths caused by looms at Amoskeag Manufacturing Company. She invented a safety device for the looms that stopped the dangerous machines from running when something did not work properly. Margaret's invention saved many lives.

Find other 19th-century inventions that were created by New Hampshire people. How did the inventions improve living and working conditions?

Elias Howe

New Hampshire Inspirations

LESSON ③ KEY IDEA REVIEW

1. What was the Industrial Revolution?
2. What are textile mills?
3. Why did mill girls return to the farms?

Go to the Source

"Little Girl" Photo

Photographer Lewis Wickes Hine took this photo of a little girl working in the Amoskeag Manufacturing Company. The company was known for making textiles, guns, shoes, trains, and sewing machines. Look at the photo carefully and answer the questions below.

Go to the Source

LOOK

What does it look like the girl is helping to make?

THINK

Do you think the girl had time to go to school?

DECIDE

Do you think it was right for children to work in mills to help their families?

Spotlighting Geography | The Louisiana Purchase

In 1803, the United States purchased a large amount of land from France. This was known as the Louisiana Purchase. Look at the map of the United States on page 270 and the map of the Louisiana Purchase below to answer the questions.

1. How many states are a result of the Louisiana Purchase?
2. List the states that came about because of the Louisiana Purchase.
3. What fraction of our present-day United States was obtained because of the Louisiana Purchase?

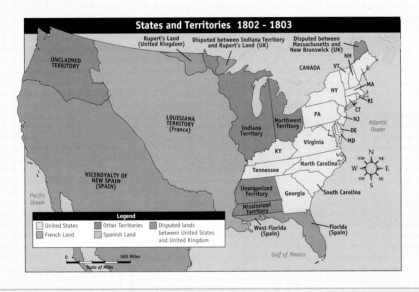

States and Territories 1802 - 1803

Reviewing the Big Idea

1. Name one problem that occurred because of the freedom of the colony.
2. In what war did the Americans and British fight over land and trading rights?
3. Compare transportation during this period to transportation today.
4. What was the Industrial Revolution?
5. Who did the Industrial Revolution affect the most? Why?
6. In your own words, restate the Big Idea of this chapter.

Becoming a Better Reader | Recognize Cause and Effect

You are learning that good readers use several strategies to help them understand new information. One of these strategies is recognizing cause and effect. Almost every event has a cause or reason behind it. Choose an event from the chapter such as the War of 1812. Write the event and its cause. Write about the cause and effect of the event in a complete paragraph including a topic sentence and three or four supporting sentences.

Civil War and Reconstruction

Big Idea

How did slavery, the economy, and states' rights lead to the Civil War?

One of the most famous Civil War battles was at Gettysburg, Pennsylvania. It was also one of the bloodiest battles. For three days, soldiers fought there, including many from New Hampshire. What is happening in this painting of the Battle of Gettysburg? What does it tell you about how wars were fought back then?

Timeline of Events

1850   1855   1860

1861
Abraham Lincoln becomes the 16th president of United States.

1853
Franklin Pierce becomes the 14th president of the United States.

1863
The Emancipation Proclamation is passed.

The second half of the 19th century brought many changes to New Hampshire and the rest of the United States. Questions about slavery and states' rights pulled the nation into a brutal civil war. Thousands of Americans died in the fighting. It took many years for the country to rebuild itself when the bloody war ended.

1861–1865
The Civil War

1877
Wood pulp is used to
make paper in Berlin.

| 1865 | 1870 | 1875 | 1880 |

1865
- Reconstruction begins.
- President Abraham Lincoln is assassinated.
- The 13th Amendment outlaws slavery in the United States.

177

Why did many people believe so strongly in slavery?

Words to Understand

abolitionist
debate
entitle
network
Underground Railroad

"In most of us colored folks was the great desire to [be] able to read and write. The greater part of the plantation owners were very harsh if we were caught trying to learn or write. . . . We could run away, but what then?"

—*John W. Fields, an enslaved man*

A National Problem

Many changes took place in New Hampshire and the rest of the United States in the 19th century. New states and territories were added to the country, new kinds of transportation and communication were developed, and new businesses were formed. The country also had problems. One of the biggest problems was slavery.

Enslaved men and women worked many hours every day. If the slaves in this picture were having a conversation, what do you think they would be saying?

The Growing Debate

Many Americans felt slavery was wrong. They wanted to make it illegal in the United States. These people were called *abolitionists*. They believed all Americans should enjoy freedoms promised in the Declaration of Independence.

Other Americans believed they were *entitled* to own slaves. Plantation owners in Southern states depended on slaves to plant, tend, and harvest thousands of acres of cotton. They sold cotton to factories in the United States and Europe. Factory owners depended on Southern cotton to make fabrics to sell around the world.

These two points of view caused a growing *debate* in the country.

Slavery in New Hampshire

Many of New Hampshire's slaves had been freed after the American Revolution. Slavery had become unpopular in the state. In 1775, there were 626 slaves in New Hampshire. By the mid-1800s, there were none.

But many New Hampshire businesses, like Amoskeag Manufacturing Company, depended on Southern cotton for making textiles. It was much cheaper to import cotton from the South than from other countries.

Southerners depended on slave labor to make money. What crop is shown in this picture? Why was this crop so important?

NEW HAMPSHIRE PORTRAIT

FRANKLIN PIERCE
1804–1869

One man from New Hampshire did not take either side of the slavery issue. He believed slavery was wrong, but he wanted states to decide on slavery. This man was Franklin Pierce. He is the only president of the United States from our state.

Franklin Pierce was elected to the state legislature when he was only 24 years old.

Franklin married and had three boys. Two of them died when they were very young.

Franklin later served in the U.S. legislature. He fought in a war against Mexico and was later elected president. Voters elected him because he was neutral in the debate over slavery. Right before he took office, his son was killed in a railroad accident.

Franklin added new territories to the country. Since many of the new regions had slaves, some people accused President Pierce of supporting slavery. He did not serve a second term as president. He returned to Concord and lived there for the rest of his life.

The Underground Railroad A Way to Freedom

Many slaves escaped from Southern plantations. They traveled to Northern states and to Canada, where slavery was not allowed. Abolitionists secretly helped the slaves escape to freedom using the *Underground Railroad.*

The Underground Railroad was not underground, and it was not a real railroad. It was a *network* of people and buildings throughout the United States and Canada. It helped slaves reach freedom.

Slaves traveled at night and hid during the day. Conductors were people who worked on the Underground Railroad. They gave slaves food, clothing, directions, and places to hide. Many conductors in New Hampshire provided their homes as safe places for slaves to hide and rest on their journey to Canada.

Many abolitionists helped slaves escape on the Underground Railroad. The enslaved people in this picture have just arrived at a station. How did they travel there?

ROUTES TO FREEDOM

CANADA

Boston
Detroit
Erie
Chicago
Philadelphia
Pittsburgh
Cincinnati
Alexandria
Parkersburg
St. Louis

Memphis

Charleston

Atlantic
Ocean

Houston • New Orleans

Gulf of Mexico

THE
BAHAMAS

MEXICO

CUBA

Legend
General routes of escape
Slave state—slavery permitted
Free state—slavery illegal

"I looked at my hands to see if I was the same person now I was free. There was such a glory over everything . . . I felt like I was in heaven."
—Harriet Tubman, a conductor on the Underground Railroad

"Whenever I hear anyone arguing for slavery, I feel a strong impulse to see it tried on him personally."
—Abraham Lincoln

$200
REWARD
Ran away from the subscriber, living eight
city of Baltimore, on the Falls Turnp
Friday, the 21st of
NEGROES
RICHARD & J

Code Words and Secret Messages

It was illegal to work for or travel on the Underground Railroad. Punishment was severe for those caught running away or helping others to escape. People used special words and phrases to hide what they were doing:

- **AGENT:** A person who arranges for safe passage of runaway slaves.
- **BRAKEMAN:** A person who helps slaves find work and homes in free states or Canada.
- **FREEDOM TRAIN:** The Underground Railroad.
- **HEAVEN**: What runaway slaves called Canada.
- **PASSENGER:** A runaway slave.
- **STATION:** A house, barn, or safe building.

This is a 19th-century painting of slaves washing diamonds in Brazil. Why do you think there are men sitting on chairs?

SLAVERY WORLDWIDE

The United States was not the only nation in the world that allowed slavery. Almost everybody living today has ancestors who were once slaves. All the ancient peoples of the world, including the Egyptians, Hebrews, Greeks, Romans, and Native Americans, had slaves.

Most historians believe slavery started as a result of war. At first, soldiers who won battles probably killed their prisoners. But then they decided to use the prisoners as slaves. People who could not pay their debts were also enslaved.

In the 19th century, people around the world questioned the existence of slavery. In the early part of the century, Latin American countries outlawed slavery. In 1833, England ended slavery in the countries it controlled. In 1848, France freed its slaves. During the next 20 years, nations looked toward the United States. They wondered how a country that believed in the Declaration of Independence could support slavery.

Slavery did not end easily in our country. It took a long, bloody fight and an amendment to the Constitution to finally abolish the practice.

LESSON ① KEY IDEA REVIEW

1. Why did some people feel like they had to have slaves?
2. What did abolitionists do?
3. What was the Underground Railroad?

A House Divided

By the middle of the 19th century, Northern states had many large cities and hundreds of factories. The South's economy depended on farming and slavery.

Most Northern states had outlawed slavery, and many Northerners wanted to end slavery throughout the United States. The Southern states wanted to expand slavery. The slavery question divided the growing country.

Civil War

The slavery debate caused many arguments among political leaders. Northern states and Southern states began operating like two different countries. This debate brought up another question: If states did not agree with laws the national government made, could they leave the Union (the United States) and form their own countries with new governments?

No one had answers that would make everyone happy. In 1861, debates over these questions erupted into the bloody Civil War.

Key Idea

What disagreement started the Civil War?

Words to Understand

assassinate
emancipation
indenture
Reconstruction
secede

"A house divided against itself cannot stand. I believe this government cannot endure permanently, half slave and half free. It will become all one thing, or all the other."

—Abraham Lincoln

The Civil War was the biggest war ever fought on American soil. This illustration shows a battle in Virginia. Which side do you think is the North? Which side do you think is the South?

A New President

When Abraham Lincoln became president of the United States, many Southern states decided to leave the Union. They believed the new president would not protect the South's interests. The states *seceded,* or left, the Union and formed a separate government. They called their government the Confederate States of America, or the Confederacy, and elected Jefferson Davis as their president.

Lincoln did not believe Southern states should be allowed to leave the United States. He did not want Americans to fight against other Americans in war, but he knew war was needed to keep the United States together as one nation.

Abraham Lincoln was our 16th president. What do you already know about him?

"If I could save the Union without freeing any slave I would do it, and if I could save it by freeing all the slaves I would do it and if I could save it by freeing some and leaving others alone I would also do that."

—Abraham Lincoln in a letter to Horace Greeley

New Hampshire in the Civil War

No Civil War battles were fought in New Hampshire, but the state's factories made shoes, clothing, and weapons for Union soldiers. Farms produced tobacco and wool to send to the battlefields.

New Hampshire also sent thousands of soldiers to fight in Civil War battles across America. For most men, it was the only time they had ever been more than a few miles from their homes.

One brave soldier from New Hampshire was Sergeant William Wilcox of Lempster. After other officers in Sergeant Wilcox's troop were wounded during a battle in Virginia, he took command of his troop and bravely finished the battle. Later, he was separated from his men, but he continued to fight with another troop of soldiers. Sergeant Wilcox was a hero of the Union army. He received the Congressional Medal of Honor, which is the highest award a soldier can receive.

What kind of volunteers is this poster trying to find?

Letters Home

Edward Hall was a New Hampshire soldier during the Civil War and wrote many letters to his wife, Susan, and his son, Eddie. His letters often told about the loneliness of war and the difficulty of being far away from family.

AUGUST 13, 1861

I miss you more and more every day and when I think how unlikely it is that we shall ever meet again it makes me sad, and Eddie, too. I want to see him very much. Give my love to him and tell him to . . . be a good boy, and remember his father.

Linking the Present to the Past

Soldiers left New Hampshire to fight in Civil War battles far from home. Many were gone for years. Letters were usually the only way to communicate with family and friends. How do New Hampshire soldiers stationed in foreign countries today keep in touch with those they leave behind?

Photographing the Civil War

Photos taken during the Civil War show us how soldiers lived, what their uniforms looked like, and the types of weapons they used.

Henry P. Moore of Concord was a photographer during the Civil War. Like many young men, he traveled to battlefields in South Carolina and Georgia. But instead of carrying a gun, Henry Moore carried a camera. He photographed many New Hampshire soldiers, giving us a view of military life in the Union army.

Soldiers often wrote and sang songs that told about battles or feelings of homesickness. Walter Kittredge, a soldier from Merrimack, became a famous songwriter during the Civil War. His most popular song was called "Tenting on the Old Campground." Read the words, and imagine you are a soldier who has just fought in a long, hard battle.

We're tenting tonight on the old Campground.
Give us a song to cheer
Our weary hearts, a song of home,
And friends we love so dear.

CHORUS
Many are the hearts that are weary tonight,
Wishing for the war to cease;
Many are the hearts looking for the right
To see the dawn of peace.
Dying tonight,
Dying tonight,
Dying on the old Campground.

Women in the Civil War

New Hampshire women were important to the Union army during the Civil War. They kept homes, farms, and businesses operating. They volunteered as nurses and spies. Many kept diaries or wrote letters about their experiences. Their writings give us another clue about life during the war.

Sarah Low

Sarah Low worked as a nurse in a hospital in Washington, D.C., during the war. She worked long hours in terrible conditions for almost three years. Day after day, hundreds of wounded or dying young men were carried into the hospital. Sarah kept a small diary of the terrible things she saw.

Nearly opposite my table lies a man who will die tonight.
He was brought in 2 or 3 weeks ago wounded through
the lungs. Farther down the ward is another surrounded
by his friends. He cannot live many days.

Even when she wasn't working, Sarah suffered many miserable things:

We should get through the nights nicely if it were not
for mosquitoes and bed-bugs, the last we have countless

*number of. Mice we do not mind, the rats I do not like . . .
they are so very large.*

Sometimes Sarah found small moments of hope:

*Last evening I sat down by a young boy who has been shot
in the foot. His name was Charlie and he was suffering a
good deal. I was surprised to find he could not read . . .
I am going to give him a reading lesson and show him
some pictures.*

A Giant Balloon

During the war, Thaddeus Lowe from Coos County built a balloon and flew it more than 500 miles from Ohio to South Carolina. President Lincoln asked Lowe to create a fleet of balloons that would allow Union soldiers to fly above their Confederate enemies and spy on them. By 1863, Lowe and his helpers had made more than 3,000 balloon flights over enemy territory. Their ability to fly high in the air gave the Union important information about enemy troop positions.

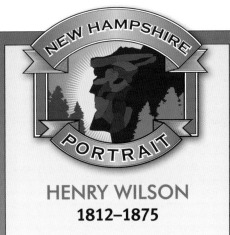
HENRY WILSON
1812–1875

Jeremiah Jones Colbath was born in Farmington and later changed his name to Henry Wilson. He was *indentured* to a farmer when he was 10 years old. For 11 years, he worked without pay. When he turned 21, he was given some oxen and six sheep, and was released from his indenture. He sold the animals and moved to Massachusetts.

During his life, Henry worked as a teacher and a shoemaker, and served as a member of Congress and a U.S. senator. During the Civil War, he commanded a group of soldiers from Massachusetts. After the war, Wilson was elected vice president of the United States under Ulysses S. Grant. He died while serving in that office.

Emancipation Proclamation

On January 1, 1863, President Abraham Lincoln signed the Emancipation Proclamation. *Emancipation* means freedom. The document stated that all slaves in Southern states were free. Confederate leaders ignored the proclamation. Since the South had seceded from the Union, Southerners didn't obey U.S. laws.

The Emancipation Proclamation allowed black men to become soldiers in the Union army and navy. After the proclamation was issued, ending slavery became a major goal of the war.

The End of the War

After many years of fighting, the North won the war, and two important questions about our national and state governments had been answered. First, the 13th Amendment was added to the U.S. Constitution. It outlawed slavery. Second, states did not have the right to secede from the United States. They could not separate to form their own countries.

For the soldiers who survived the war, the end of the fighting meant they could go home. Families and friends who had been separated for years were finally reunited.

More than 10,000 battles were fought across the United States during the Civil War. More than 600,000 Americans died fighting.

What Do You Think?

How was the Civil War helpful to our nation? How was it hurtful?

LIFE IN POETRY

These poems were written by New Hampshire poets during the 1800s. Read the biographies of the two poets and think about how life in the United States during the mid-1800s influenced their writing. How does the first poem, which was written before the Civil War, make you feel? How does the second poem, which was written after the war, make you feel?

James Monroe Whitfield

James Monroe Whitfield was born in New Hampshire to free black parents in 1822. During his lifetime, there were few work opportunities for free black men. He moved to Buffalo, New York, and worked as a barber. Whitfield wrote poems to promote the end of slavery in the United States before the Civil War.

Celia Laighton Thaxter

Celia Thaxter was born in Portsmouth in 1835 and moved to the Isles of Shoals when her father was appointed lighthouse keeper there. Her island home provided a quiet, pleasant place for Thaxter to live and write after the Civil War.

"Yes! Strike Again That Sounding String"
by James M. Whitfield

Sing not to me of landscapes bright,
Of fragrant flowers and fruitful trees—
Of azure skies and mellow light,
Or whisperings of the gentle breeze;

But tell me of the tempest roaring
Across the angry foaming deep,
Or torrents from the mountains pouring
Down precipices dark and steep.

Sing of the lightning's lurid flash,
The ocean's roar, the howling storm,
The earthquake's shock, the thunder's crash,
Where ghastly terrors teeming swarm . . .

"The Sandpiper"
by Celia Thaxter

Across the lonely beach we flit,
One little sandpiper and I,
And fast I gather, bit by bit,
The scattered drift-wood, bleached and dry.
The wild waves reach their hands for it,
The wild wind raves, the tide runs high,
As up and down the beach we flit,
One little sandpiper and I.

Above our heads the sullen clouds
Scud, black and swift, across the sky:
Like silent ghosts in misty shrouds
Stand out the white light-houses high.
Almost as far as eye can reach
I see the close-reefed vessels fly,
As fast we flit along the beach,
One little sandpiper and I.

Reconstruction

After the Civil War ended, the Northern and Southern states had to find ways to work together as a united nation. *Reconstruction* was a time of rebuilding the country in the years following the war. A few Reconstruction efforts began even before the war was over.

During Reconstruction, leaders decided how to bring Southern states back into the Union. They decided which rights would be granted to the four million freed slaves. They decided how cities, railroads, and factories in the South would be rebuilt and who would pay for the work.

After the Civil War ended, black people were given their right to vote. Why would they be happy about this?

Results of Reconstruction

The Reconstruction period lasted for more than 12 years. Several good things resulted from the efforts of national leaders during that time.

- The 13th Amendment was added to the U.S. Constitution. It outlawed slavery.
- Each of the Confederate states rejoined the Union and began reforming their own state governments.
- Black men were given the right to vote.

Many bad things also resulted from the long years of Reconstruction.

- Most Southern whites refused to accept blacks as equal.
- Blacks were free, but they were poor and had little political power.
- Although black men were allowed to vote, many whites used violence and threats to keep them from voting.

After the war, many African Americans left the farms they had worked on as slaves. Many of them went north to find jobs. Why did they want to move north?

The Death of Lincoln

President Abraham Lincoln was shot at Ford's Theatre just five days after Confederate General Robert E. Lee surrendered to Union General Ulysses S. Grant.

A man named John Wilkes Booth was angry that the South had lost the Civil War. He wanted slavery to continue in the United States. As the president watched a play from his seat above the stage, Booth shot him in the back of the head. Lincoln was the first U.S. president to be *assassinated*.

This is a drawing of Lincoln's assassination. ▲ *John Wilkes Booth was the murderer, but later it was discovered that others were involved as well. Does the picture match the story you read of the shooting?*

This newspaper is offering a reward for the people responsible for Lincoln's death. How much money is being offered? ▶

LESSON ② KEY IDEA REVIEW 🔑

1. What country did the seceded states form?
2. Explain the Emancipation Proclamation.
3. Which side won the Civil War?

Key Idea

What changes took place after the Civil War?

Words to Understand

foreman
obstacle
revival
sawmill
shanty
stock

Big Changes

The problems and big changes taking place in the United States after the war worried many people. They did not like the conflict between Northern and Southern states. They believed businesses were becoming too big and that workers were treated like machines instead of human beings. They were afraid governments were ignoring the teachings of churches.

Comfort in Religion

Many people found security and comfort in their religious beliefs. The United States experienced a growth in religious revival. A *revival* is a renewed interest in something. New Hampshire became home to several different religious groups.

Religious revivals became very common in the United States after the Civil War. Why do you think there are tents set up in the background of this picture?

The Shakers

The Shakers were a religious group that came to the United States in the late 1700s. They were founded by Ann Lee. The Shakers established several communities from Maine to Kentucky. They settled in Enfield and Canterbury in New Hampshire. They were called Shakers because they danced and shook during their worship services.

These are some Shaker beliefs and customs:

- They did not marry. They lived in their communities as brothers and sisters.
- They worked together and shared everything.
- They refused to fight in wars.
- They believed men and women were equal.
- They believed people of all races and cultures were equal.

Anyone could join a Shaker community. Children joined with their parents and were raised by the entire community. The Shakers also raised orphans. At the age of 21, a person decided whether to stay at the Shaker community or leave.

The Shakers were hard workers. Their motto was "Hands to work and hearts to God." They started many businesses and sold their products. They invented the clothespin, the flat broom, the circular saw, a washing machine, and an oven.

Church of Christ, Scientist

Mary Morse Baker Eddy was born in Bow and grew up on her father's farm. She suffered several illnesses and injuries as a young woman and spent time reading the Bible for comfort and guidance. Mary believed she could cure her illnesses and injuries by studying the works and sayings of Jesus.

From her study of the Bible, Mary began to believe all diseases could be healed through faith in God. She and others who shared her beliefs formed the Church of Christ, Scientist. Mary became pastor and "Mother" of the church. She established the church's headquarters in Boston and oversaw its activities. She founded the daily newspaper *The Christian Science Monitor* to connect her church with its followers.

Mary moved to Concord at the end of her life. She devoted her life to her church and to helping poor people.

Here are Shakers during church service. Why do you think "Shakers" was a good name for them?

Linking the Present to the Past

You can visit a New Hampshire Shaker village today in Canterbury. If you visit, you can learn how to weave baskets or make brooms!

Mary Morse Baker Eddy

Logging was extremely dangerous, hard work. What dangers do you see in this painting?

The Rise of Logging

One of the most important industries in New Hampshire after the Civil War was logging. In the 19th century, almost everything was made of wood. Loggers cut trees and delivered them to **sawmills** to be cut into lumber.

Logging companies used rivers and railroads to move logs to sawmills and paper companies. The Androscoggin and Connecticut rivers were important in the logging industry.

Logging was dangerous work. Many men were crushed by falling trees or sleds they used to move heavy logs. Some drowned while guiding logs down rivers.

Lumber Camp

Each fall, loggers set up a lumber camp. They built **shanties,** or temporary homes, to live in throughout the coming winter months.

Each shanty had a large fireplace for cooking and heat. Sleeping bunks with straw mattresses lined the shanty walls. Loggers sat on their bunks or on log benches to eat their meals. Wives and children did not live in lumber camps.

Payday

Many of the men in the logging camps could not read, write, or speak English. Loggers wore a numbered metal tag so they could be identified. On payday, each man showed his tag to the foreman to receive his wages. The tags also helped identify men who were hurt or lost.

Jobs at Camp

It took a lot of work to keep a lumber camp working. Let's look at some of the loggers' jobs:

Cooks: Loggers had big appetites. Cooks prepared big meals to keep all the men fed. They cooked beans for each meal since they did not spoil quickly and were easy to transport. They also served milk, eggs, beef, and potatoes.

Foremen: The men in charge of logging operations were called *foremen*. They made sure each man did his work. They cared for those who were sick or injured, kept track of the camp's supplies, broke up fights, and settled arguments. They also issued paychecks.

Choppers: Choppers cut down the trees. They knew how to strike their axes to make the trees fall in just the right direction. This kept the men safe and allowed the horses or oxen to easily pull the fallen trees out of the forest.

Skidders and Teamsters: Skidders hauled the logs out of the woods. They attached a chain from the animal harness to each log. Sleds underneath the logs helped the animals pull the heavy trees over snow and ice. Teamsters took care of the horses and oxen.

River Drivers: River drivers drove logs downriver to sawmills. During the first weeks of a log drive, more than 500 men worked as river drivers. They were divided up into groups of about 50, each working under a different boss. The men worked for months, often 16 hours a day, to move hundreds of logs downriver.

Logs are very heavy, and it took strong horses to pull loads like this one. How do you think loggers transport logs today?

Log jams like this one were very dangerous. What do you think would happen if this jam suddenly cleared?

On big drives down large rivers, timber was tied together to form rafts. Men built huts on the rafts and ate and slept on them instead of setting up tents beside the river.

Log Jams

Curves and other *obstacles* in a river often caused logs to jam. Once a few got stuck, others quickly collected behind them. River drivers had to climb onto the log jam and work logs free. Once free, the logs moved fast. The men had to scramble to get back to shore before the water's current pulled them under.

Life in a Logging Camp

This account of logging was written by Reverend Orrin Robbins Hunt, who lived in a logging camp in Pittsburg.

These camps are very warm and comfortable, and under the supervision of a good cook are kept clean and orderly. The lights are put out and the men are all in bed at 9 o'clock in the evening.

At 5 o'clock [in the morning] the cook has his biscuits made, and the breakfast is ready. It consists of baked beans, hot biscuits, sweetbread, doughnuts, dried apple sauce, molasses, and tea. The other meals are varied each day, although baked beans are always on the table for those who wish for them, and they are preferred by many.

In this camp, where it was my privilege to stop, we had teamsters, road men, landing men, choppers, swampers, and yarders. The choppers fell the trees, the swampers clear the way to them, and the yarders drag the logs to the yard where the teamsters load.

Sawmills

The first sawmills in New Hampshire were built near the woods where trees were felled. Later, bigger mills were built along rivers so logs could be floated down to them. Sawmills usually operated in the spring and summer months.

Loggers used long poles to push logs toward the mill. A large waterwheel pulled each log into the mill. Another wheel pushed out the cut lumber.

Uses of Lumber

Sawmills cut wood into different sizes and shapes. Long, thin planks were best for building homes. Gunsmiths used lumber to carve *stocks* for guns. Wheelwrights used wood to make wagon wheels. Coopers used wood for barrels. Even musical instrument makers depended on wood supplied by sawmills.

Look at this picture carefully. Why was it important for sawmills to be built on rivers?

LESSON ③ KEY IDEA REVIEW

1. Why did people turn to religion after the Civil War?
2. Why was the logging industry so important?
3. List the five jobs that were available at a lumber camp.

Logging Railroads

Railroads provided another way to carry heavy logs to sawmills. Trains were so successful in transporting lumber that logging companies began to clear thousands of acres of forest land. Citizens in the state were concerned about how fast the forests were being destroyed. They formed organizations to limit the number and types of trees loggers could remove.

What Do You Think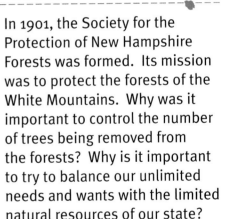

In 1901, the Society for the Protection of New Hampshire Forests was formed. Its mission was to protect the forests of the White Mountains. Why was it important to control the number of trees being removed from the forests? Why is it important to try to balance our unlimited needs and wants with the limited natural resources of our state?

After the invention of the circular saw in the mid-1800s, the process of cutting logs into lumber became faster than ever before.

"New Hampshire": A Poem
by John Greenleaf Whittier

God bless New Hampshire! for her granite peaks
Once more the voice of Stark and Langdon speaks.
The long-bound vassal of the exulting South
For very shame her self-forged chain has broken;
Torn the black seal of slavery from her mouth
And in the clear tones of her old time spoken!
Oh, all undreamed of, all unhoped for changes!
The tyrant's ally proves his sternest foe;
To all his biddings, from her mountain ranges,
New Hampshire thunders an indignant No!
Who is it now despairs? Oh, faint of heart,
Look upward to those Northern mountains cold,
Flouted by freedom's victor-flag unrolled,
And gather strength to bear a manlier part!
All is not lost. The angel of God's blessing
Encamps with Freedom on the field of fight;
Still to her banner, day by day, are pressing
Unlooked for allies, striking for the right!
Courage, then, Northern hearts! Be firm, be true;
What one brave State hath done, can ye not also do?

Go to the Source

LOOK	THINK	DECIDE
In the second line, Whittier mentions "Stark and Langdon." Why are these men important to our state?	What do you think this poem is taking a courageous stand against?	Why does Whittier refer to New Hampshire as a "brave state"?

CHAPTER REVIEW

Spotlighting Geography | Civil War Map

Look at this Civil War America map and answer the questions.

1. How many slave states (Confederate) are shown on the map?
2. How many free states and territories (Union) are shown on the map?
3. What types of states border New Hampshire?

Civil War America

WASHINGTON TERRITORY
OR
NEVADA TERRITORY
CA
UTAH TERRITORY
DAKOTA TERRITORY
COLORADO TERRITORY
NEBRASKA TERRITORY
NEW MEXICO TERRITORY
INDIAN TERRITORY
KS
MN
IA
WI
MI
IL
IN
OH
MO
KY
Tennessee
Arkansas
Texas
Louisiana
Mississippi
Alabama
Georgia
North Carolina
South Carolina
Virginia
PA
NY
VT
NH
ME
MA
RI
CT
NJ
DE
MD
Florida
CANADA
MEXICO
Atlantic Ocean
Pacific Ocean
Gulf of Mexico

Legend
Union States
Confederate States
Border States
Union-held Territories

0   500 Miles
Scale of Miles

Reviewing the Big Idea

1. What were the names of the two sides fighting in the Civil War?
2. Describe New Hampshire's point of view on slavery in your own words.
3. Why is the Emancipation Proclamation a significant document in our history?
4. Think of a person today who fights for what he or she believes in. Compare and contrast this person with an abolitionist from the mid-1800s.
5. List two things that were a result of Reconstruction.
6. Describe what the United States might be like today if the Civil War had never happened.

Becoming a Better Reader | Recognize Point of View

You may have heard, "Everyone is entitled to their opinion." While this is true, it is important to base your opinions on facts. Even with the same facts, people will have different opinions. Every person has a different viewpoint on important issues. A viewpoint is the way someone thinks about something. Someone's viewpoint is affected by where they live, how they were raised, by their education, and many other factors. Good readers recognize what is fact or opinion and how opinions are formed based on a person's viewpoint. Choose an idea from this chapter that people have different opinions about. Write a couple of sentences about the idea from two different points of view.

Big Idea

How did immigrants, wars, and new technology change life in New Hampshire and the United States?

This woman is using a bell jar to help with a science experiment at the Vacuum Bell Treatment Center in Concord. Why do you think they call the glass cover a bell jar?

Timeline of Events

New Hampshire in the 20th Century and Beyond

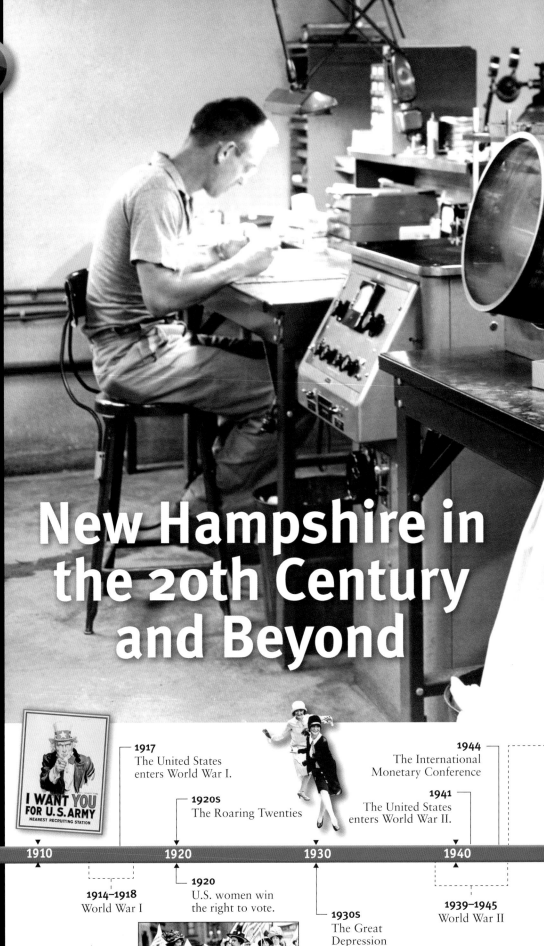

I WANT YOU FOR U.S. ARMY
NEAREST RECRUITING STATION

1917
The United States enters World War I.

1920S
The Roaring Twenties

1944
The International Monetary Conference

1941
The United States enters World War II.

1910   1920   1930   1940

1914–1918
World War I

1920
U.S. women win the right to vote.

1930S
The Great Depression

1939–1945
World War II

During the 20th century, life in the United States changed in many ways. There were many wars and many years when it was difficult to earn a living. There were new inventions and new ideas. There were new ways of thinking about our freedoms and rights as American citizens. The 21st century continues to bring new challenges and opportunities to our state and nation.

1945–1989
The Cold War

1960s–1975
U.S. troops involved in the Vietnam War

1986
The space shuttle *Challenger* explodes.

2001
- Terrorists attack the United States.
- The United States declares the "War on Terror."
- U.S. soldiers are sent to fight in Afghanistan.

1954–1968
The Civil Rights Movement

| 1950 | 1960 | 1970 | 1980 | 1990 | 2000 |

1950–1953
The Korean War

1964
The Civil Rights Act is created.

1969
U.S. astronauts land on the moon.

2002
Creation of Department of Homeland Security

2003
The United States sends soldiers to fight in Iraq.

2008
Our state joins the Regional Greenhouse Gas Initiative.

Key Idea

How did immigrants and new technology change life in New Hampshire and the United States?

Words to Understand

image
launch
opportunity
resident
satellite
technology

What Do You Think?

Why do you think Emma Lazarus's poem was chosen for the Statue of Liberty? How would you feel as an immigrant reading these words?

New People in a New Century

People emigrated from all over the world to make their homes in the United States during the 20th century.

They came from Canada, England, France, Ireland, Italy, Greece, China, Mexico, and many other nations. They came to have more rights and find jobs and better **opportunities**.

The customs, religions, and skills of the immigrants became part of American society. New inventions, medicines, and ideas helped our growing population live and work here.

During the mid-1800s, many French Canadian **residents** immigrated to our state. They mostly found work on farms, in the logging industry, and in textile mills.

The First Glimpse of America

Most new immigrants sailed into New York's harbor and saw the Statue of Liberty. The statue was a welcomed sight after long weeks on cramped ships. On the statue's base are words written by poet Emma Lazarus. Here is part of her poem titled "The New Colossus":

Give me your tired, your poor,
Your huddled masses yearning to breathe free,
The wretched refuse of your teeming shore.
Send these, the homeless, tempest-tost to me:
I lift my lamp beside the golden door!

Immigrants brought their hopes and dreams to the United States. They also brought their cultures, traditions, and languages. Here are some words we use today that came from languages used in other countries. Can you guess which immigrant groups might have brought these words to America?

- garage
- troll
- plaza
- kindergarten
- pizza
- jungle

A Century of New Inventions

At the beginning of the 20th century, most people traveled from place to place on horseback, railroad, or steamship. They communicated by letter, telegraph, and telephone.

By the end of the century, *technology* had changed. People zipped across roads in cars, soared above the ground in airplanes, and even viewed the Earth from spaceships and *satellites* thousands of miles away. Computers sent instant messages around the globe. Radio, television, and computers brought sounds and *images* into American homes. Medical knowledge had improved so scientists could study cells in the human body and prevent many deadly illnesses.

Made in New Hampshire

Many useful inventions have been created in our state. Some of these have made life easier, and some have led to other inventions. Which one in the list do you think helped with the invention of the automobile?

guitar

barbecue grill

steam power

washing machine

churn

engine

Televisions, telephones, and computers were all inventions of the 20th century. You probably use these things every day. What other 20th-century inventions do you use?

Some inventions of the 20th century changed the way we think about food! Earl Silas Tupper grew up in a New Hampshire farming family. As a young man, Tupper worked for DuPont, a company that manufactured plastics. He learned how to design and make plastic products, and then he *launched* his own company. After World War II, he invented a product called Tupperware. Tupperware containers are made of plastic and have tight lids that keep food fresh.

Maurice and Dick McDonald of Manchester opened a new kind of restaurant in California. They named their fast-food hamburger business McDonald's and promised customers would receive their food only minutes after placing orders! The McDonald brothers sold their restaurant to Ray Kroc in 1961 for just under $3 million. Since then, billions and billions have been served!

McDonald's has changed a lot since it was first started. How does this McDonald's restaurant look different from the ones you see today?

LESSON ① KEY IDEA REVIEW

1. What item was a welcoming sight for new immigrants?
2. What did immigrants bring with them to the United States?
3. How did people travel at the beginning of the 20th century?

A Century of Wars

The 20th century brought big changes in the way people viewed America's role in the world. During these years, millions of American soldiers fought in wars around the globe. New Hampshire men and women took part in the fighting. They were sent to faraway countries such as Germany, Italy, Japan, Korea, Vietnam, and Iraq. Many died to protect freedoms and liberties we enjoy as citizens of the United States. The first large war of the 20th century was called World War I.

World War I

This war started when countries began fighting one another for more land and greater power. One side in the war was called the Central Powers. It included the countries of Austria-Hungary, Bulgaria, Germany, and the Ottoman Empire. The other side was called the Allies. Some of the Allied countries were Great Britain, France, Italy, Japan, Russia, and the United States. The Allies won the war in 1918.

Key Idea

What effects did war have on Americans?

Words to Understand

Holocaust
prosperity
ration
sacrifice
stock
strike
suffragist
war bond

Soldiers wave to their families as they ride off to war. Many of them never saw their families again.

I WANT YOU
FOR U.S. ARMY
NEAREST RECRUITING STATION

Posters like this one invited men to sign up to be soldiers. The man in the tall hat is Uncle Sam. His image is based on Samuel Wilson from Mason, New Hampshire. He supplied beef to the U.S. Army in the early 1800s. What are Uncle Sam's initials? What does he represent?

The Fight for Women's Rights

After World War I ended, the United States focused on a different kind of war at home. This fight was over women's rights.

Laws in the United States had never allowed women to vote in major elections. Many people, called *suffragists*, thought this was unfair. They protested by holding meetings, marching in parades, and giving speeches demanding change. Some women even refused to eat until they were given the right to vote. Police officers threw the starving women in jail and fed them by force. All of these actions by women fighting for voting rights was called the suffrage movement.

The 19th Amendment

The suffrage movement ended in 1920, when the 19th Amendment was added to the U.S. Constitution. This amendment reads: "The right of citizens of the United States to vote shall not be denied or abridged by the United States or by any State on account of sex." American women were finally able to vote.

Look at this suffragist who is marching and protesting. What clue in the photo tells you what she is marching for?

New Hampshire Women and the 19th Amendment

Marilla Ricker

Marilla Ricker was born in New Durham. Before women were allowed to vote in the United States, she became New Hampshire's first female lawyer and even ran for governor. She believed that since she paid property taxes, she should be able to vote. She registered to vote several times, but voting officials never allowed her to vote. Just months before her death, the 19th Amendment passed, and Marilla Ricker was able to vote.

Jessie Doe and Dr. Mary Louise Rolfe Farnum were the first women elected to the New Hampshire House of Representatives. Jessie Doe represented Rollinsford. Dr. Farnum represented Boscawen. They won their elections only a few days after the ratification of the 19th Amendment.

The Roaring Twenties

Toward the end of the suffrage movement, the United States enjoyed many years of **prosperity**, or wealth. People earned higher wages than they had before the war. They bought things like houses, cars, refrigerators, radios, and telephones. They went to movie theaters and listened to a new style of music called jazz. This time was called the Roaring Twenties.

Many people used their extra money to buy shares of **stock** in companies. With a share of stock, a person owned a portion of a company. During the 1920s, many companies made a lot of money by selling shares of stock, so the price of stocks went up. Stock prices rose so high that some people began borrowing money from banks to buy stock.

These women are called flappers. They wore short skirts and short haircuts. How do they look the same or different from women today?

The Roaring Twenties meant a new way of life for many Americans. This radio might look old fashioned to you, but it was a popular item in the 1920s. Look at the photo carefully. How do you think a modern radio is better than this one?

The Great Depression

In 1929, the value of stocks dropped suddenly. Many people around the world lost all the money they had invested. They could no longer afford to buy things like cars and houses. They could not repay banks the money they had borrowed. This time was called the Great Depression.

During the Great Depression, banks around the world closed, farms failed, and factories stopped making things. Millions of people lost jobs and all their savings. In many places, there was not enough money to buy food to feed everyone. Soup kitchens gave meals to those who waited in long lines each day. The U.S. government created jobs to help Americans through the tough times. The Great Depression lasted about 10 years. It ended when a second world war began.

The End of Amoskeag Manufacturing

The Great Depression affected many towns and businesses in New Hampshire. The largest business to suffer was Amoskeag Manufacturing Company (AMC).

After World War I, AMC began losing money because of competition from mills in southern states. Southern mills had newer equipment and paid workers less money. They sold textiles for lower prices than AMC.

AMC tried to compete with southern mills by cutting workers' pay and making them work longer hours. Workers did not want less pay and longer hours. Finally, they went on *strike* and refused to work. The company lost money during the strike because it was not able to produce textiles. During the Great Depression, AMC could not sell enough textiles to pay its workers. Workers were angry. In 1933 and 1934, they held violent strikes against the company. Soldiers from the state militia were sent to Manchester to keep the peace.

AMC closed on Christmas Eve in 1935. Thousands of people lost their jobs. Everyone hoped the company would reopen the mills, but a terrible flood destroyed many of its buildings. The company never recovered.

These workers are striking at AMC because they didn't want less pay and longer hours.

THORNTON WILDER

While most of the world struggled, many artists and authors found comfort in New Hampshire. Thornton Wilder was one such author and playwright. During the Great Depression, Wilder spent time at the MacDowell Colony in Peterborough. The colony was a place where writers and other artists could live and work away from distractions of everyday life. While at the colony, Wilder was inspired to write a play called *Our Town*. The play was set in the imaginary community of Grover's Corners, New Hampshire. It told the story of ordinary people in small-town America. It has become a symbol of rural New Hampshire life.

It's early afternoon. All 2,642 have had their dinners and all the dishes have been washed. There's an early-afternoon calm in our town: a buzzin' and a hummin' from the school buildings; only a few buggies on Main Street. . . . Doc Gibbs is in his office, tapping people and making them say "ah." Mr. Webb's cuttin' his lawn over there; one man in ten thinks it's a privilege to push his own lawn mower.

—*Our Town, Act I*

EDMUND TARBELL

By the beginning of the 20th century, Edmund Tarbell was one of America's most popular artists. He spent summers in New Castle and moved there in the last years of his life. He painted in a style known as Impressionism, often using his wife or daughters as subjects. His paintings showed people and nature in peaceful scenes.

I'm Proud... my husband wants me to do my part

SEE YOUR U. S. EMPLOYMENT SERVICE
WAR MANPOWER COMMISSION

Posters like this encouraged women to get jobs to help the war effort. Why do you think they were effective?

Would you like to learn more about the Holocaust? The Cohen Center for Holocaust Studies at Keene State College teaches all about this tragic event.

These men were prisoners during the Holocaust. How do you think they were feeling?

World War II

The largest war of the 20th century was called World War II. The United States, England, France, and other countries (known as the Allies) fought against Germany, Italy, and Japan. Fathers and sons left their New Hampshire homes and went to foreign countries to fight.

Many mothers and daughters took jobs in factories to keep the country and state operating. The women operated machines that made airplanes, ships, and guns to supply the Allied war efforts. New Hampshire factories aided the war effort by making boots, uniforms, and gas masks, and shipyards built submarines and destroyers for the U.S. Navy.

Other women served in the military as nurses, office clerks, and instructors. Some were pilots and flew new military airplanes from factories to military bases.

The Holocaust

During the long years of World War II, German soldiers under the command of Adolf Hitler murdered nearly 11 million innocent men, women, and children. More than half of those killed were Jewish people. This terrible event is known as the *Holocaust*.

Hitler wanted to control the entire world. He wanted everyone to agree with decisions he made about religion, jobs, families, and government. He believed killing everyone who did not agree with him would help him achieve his goal.

Children and World War II

American soldiers needed guns, trucks, ships, food, and many other things to help them win the war.

If you were a child during World War II, you would have made many sacrifices to help in the war effort. **Sacrifice** means to go without things you want or need.

Your family might not have had enough gasoline to run its car during the war. The gasoline was needed for military tanks, planes, and jeeps. Butter, sugar, shoes, and coats were also difficult to get. These things had to be **rationed**. That means people were able to buy them only in limited amounts.

You might have helped American soldiers by collecting old automobile tires and tin cans. Factories recycled the rubber and metal to make weapons, trucks, and warships.

Another way you might have helped in the war effort was to save your pennies. You could take them to school and buy special stamps sold by the government. Then you pasted your stamps in a savings booklet. When the booklet's pages were filled, you could exchange it at the post office for a **war bond**. The government used your pennies to buy things like guns, tents, helmets, and tools for our soldiers. After the war, you could return your war bond to the government. You would get your money back—plus a little more!

Strawbery Banke in Portsmouth preserves the Marden-Abbott House and Store, which supplied food during the war. To learn more about the war and its effect on American life, visit the Wright Museum in Wolfeboro.

This poster is meant to encourage people to buy war bonds. The shadow you see was the symbol for the German army. What clue in the picture tells you these children are American?

Don't Let That Shadow Touch Them
Buy WAR BONDS

The man on the left is a prisoner-of-war woodsman. What kind of work do you think he has to do?

German Prisoner-of-War Camp

During World War II, the United States created 500 prisoner-of-war camps across the country. A prisoner of war is an enemy soldier who has been captured. A camp was a type of prison where the enemy soldiers were kept.

Camp Stark opened in the town of Stark, which was named after General John Stark. He introduced our state motto, "Live Free or Die." This camp was our state's only prisoner-of-war camp. More than 250 enemy soldiers were held there during the war. These men were put to work cutting down trees and hauling them to local paper mills. Camp Stark closed at the end of the war, and the prisoners were released.

NEW HAMPSHIRE PORTRAIT

RENE GAGNON
1925–1979

Rene Gagnon was a teenager living in Manchester when World War II started. He joined the marines when he was 17 years old.

Rene became famous during World War II for something that happened on an island called Iwo Jima. He and five other men struggled to raise the American flag. A photographer named Joe Rosenthal took pictures of them. One of those pictures became the most famous photograph of World War II. It became a national symbol for the United States.

Rene Gagnon returned to Manchester after the war ended and went to work in the textile mills. He is buried in Arlington National Cemetery, outside Washington, D.C.

This is a photo of the Bretton Woods International Monetary Conference. What clues in the photo tell you that many countries took part in the conference?

The End of World War II

In 1945, the Allies won World War II when Germany surrendered. Japan surrendered a few months later.

Many countries in Europe and Asia had been destroyed during the war. Now it was time to repair the damage. New Hampshire played an important role in rebuilding the war-torn countries.

Bretton Woods International Monetary Conference

Before the end of World War II, 730 leaders from around the globe met at a hotel in Bretton Woods. Their meeting was called the United Nations Monetary and Financial Conference.

The leaders wanted to help countries rebuild after the war, but there was a problem. All the countries used different kinds of money. This made it hard to buy and sell goods between countries. At the conference, the leaders decided all countries would use the U.S. dollar to measure how much things cost. Now it was easier for countries to trade goods and services.

Portsmouth's Submarines

Half of the American submarines used in World War II were designed at the Portsmouth Naval Shipyard. After the war ended, the shipyard continued to build submarines.

LESSON ② KEY IDEA REVIEW

1. Why is the 19th Amendment important?
2. Name three things that happened during the Great Depression.
3. How did Americans help during World War II?

The Civil Rights Movement

In the early 1950s, many Americans began a new fight. This one was for civil rights. **Civil Rights** are the freedoms and powers people have as members of communities, states, or nations. The U.S. Constitution guarantees citizens civil rights such as freedom of speech, freedom of the press, and freedom of religion. We also have the right to own property. Every American has the right to receive equal treatment.

For almost 200 years, these civil rights were not enjoyed by all Americans. Slavery ended in the 19th century, but laws did not allow black Americans the same rights as white Americans. Black children could not go to the same schools as white children. Black families could not live in "white" neighborhoods. Some drinking fountains were "Blacks Only," and others were "Whites Only."

Many people wanted the unfair treatment to end. These people participated in the Civil Rights Movement. Hundreds were arrested for speaking out about their beliefs, and some were killed.

Many places had separate bathrooms, drinking fountains, and other services for black people. What does the sign in the picture mean?

The Civil Rights Movement led to the creation of the Civil Rights Act of 1964. This act made it illegal to treat people differently based on things like skin color and gender.

Dr. Martin Luther King Jr.

One man who was influential in gaining civil rights for all Americans was Dr. Martin Luther King Jr. He was an African American minister and leader of the Civil Rights Movement. King used his skills as a public speaker to encourage Americans to demand equal rights. He believed people could fight for change without using violence. Not everyone agreed with him, though, and he was murdered on April 4, 1968, in Memphis, Tennessee.

A Time of Change

The 20th century brought many changes to our state and nation. Tourism, technology, and important goods and sevices had made New Hampshire much wealthier. As the century ended, people looked forward to another period of progress and change.

JONATHAN DANIELS
1939–1965

Before Dr. Martin Luther King Jr. was killed, he asked American college students to meet him in Selma, Alabama. King was planning a civil rights march to the state capital in Montgomery.

Jonathan Myrick Daniels, of Keene, went to Selma and joined the march. He was impressed by King's work and later returned to Alabama to continue the push for civil rights. At one point, Jonathan was arrested for supporting the Civil Rights Movement.

After his release from jail, Jonathan tried to enter a store in Alabama. A man with a gun stopped him and told him to leave. The man then aimed the gun at a young girl standing next to Jonathan. Jonathan pushed the girl out of the way just as the man fired. Jonathan was hit by the bullet and died instantly.

NEW HAMPSHIRE'S Outer Space Connection

The 20th century was not just about wars. During this time, our country was part of an exciting race! In the late 1950s, the United States became involved in the "space race." We wanted to be the first country to send someone to outer space. Many people from New Hampshire were involved in the space program.

ALAN B. SHEPARD

Alan B. Shepard was born on a farm in East Derry. When he was 10 years old, he got a job delivering newspapers on Saturday mornings. He bought a bike with the money he earned and often rode it to the local airport to watch planes take off and land.

As a young man, Shepard attended the United States Naval Academy. His navy career started on a ship in the Pacific Ocean during World War II. Later, he became an airplane test pilot and a fighter pilot. He logged more than 8,000 hours of flying time.

Shepard was selected to be one of the *Mercury* astronauts for NASA. He became the first American to travel into space and the fifth to walk on the moon.

CHRISTA MCAULIFFE

Sharon Christa McAuliffe, the oldest of five children, was born in Boston, Massachusetts. She became a social studies teacher at Concord High School in New Hampshire and was selected by NASA for the Teacher in Space program. She was selected out of 11,500 applicants to become the first teacher to ever fly on a space shuttle mission.

On January 28, 1986, just 73 seconds after liftoff, the space shuttle *Challenger* exploded, killing Christa and the six other astronauts on board. The Christa McAuliffe Planetarium in Concord serves as a memorial to her life and work.

Space Technology on Earth

During the 20th century, Americans traveled to the moon. They also flew space shuttles around the Earth and built a space station where scientists could live and work. To make those things happen, new products and technologies were invented. Many of the inventions designed for the space program changed the way we do things right here in New Hampshire.

OTHER SPACE-AGE INVENTIONS

- You probably have nonstick pans at home. The material used on them was designed for the space program!

- Special materials that protected astronauts' space suits from fire are used in some of the clothing you wear.

- Satellites circling Earth take pictures of storms, crops, and pollution.

LESSON ③ KEY IDEA REVIEW

1. What are civil rights?
2. What was the Civil Rights Movement?
3. What was the "space race"?

Key Idea

What is life like in present-day New Hampshire?

Words to Understand

challenge
determine
global warming
Internet
partner
patent
terrorist

In October 2001, Apple introduced the iPod, a media player used to play music. How is it different than the radio shown on page 207?

The 21st Century

Thousands of people have moved into New Hampshire since the start of the 21st century. They came because of our state's good jobs, schools, people, and natural resources. They came to enjoy New Hampshire's way of life.

We must all work together to make New Hampshire an even better place to live. To do this, we will need to develop new types of technology, help our nation strengthen its relationships with other countries, and help the rest of the world in protecting our planet's environment.

New Technologies

In the first part of this chapter, we learned about some important changes in technology during the 20th century. Inventions like cars, computers, and televisions changed the way we worked and played in the past.

As we begin the 21st century, inventors continue to create new things to improve our lives. Some inventions help us to stay healthier. Others make our work easier. Have you ever listened to music on an iPod? Have you ever played a sport using a Wii? Do you text your friends? These are all examples of new technologies that people use.

The Wii is a home video game system invented by Nintendo. Do you know how it is different than other game systems?

One of the most important forms of technology is the Internet. The **Internet** is a worldwide system of connected computers. The computers work together to share information. People use the Internet to communicate with one another and to exchange ideas.

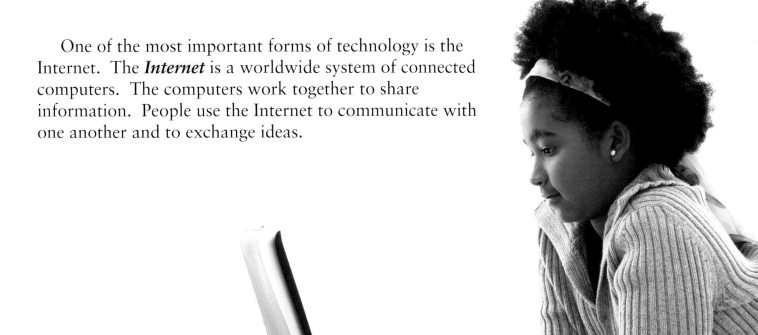

Computers and the Internet are a big part of our lives today. What do you use the Internet for? What would life be like without these inventions?

Dean Kamen, Inventor

Dean Kamen is a Bedford inventor and businessman. He holds hundreds of patents in the United States and other countries. A **patent** gives an inventor the sole right to make and earn money from his invention. Kamen created a company in Manchester that uses science and technology to invent products that allow people to live longer, healthier lives.

Dean Kamen's most famous invention is called the Segway Personal Transporter (PT). It is a two-wheeled, battery-powered machine that moves people from place to place. The Segway has no pedal or brake. Instead, the motions of its human rider power the machine and **determine** which direction it goes and how fast.

Also located in Manchester is FIRST (For Inspiration and Recognition of Science and Technology), a public charity that was founded by Dean Kamen. It designs programs that teach kids about science, technology, and math.

This is a photo of Dean Kamen on one of his inventions, the Segway. Who would this invention be useful for and why?

The War on Terror

On September 11, 2001, terrorists took control of four American airplanes. Three were crashed into buildings in the United States and a fourth plane crashed in a field in Pennsylvania. *Terrorists* are people who use violence or threats to make other people do things terrorists want them to do. People often refer to the 2001 attacks on America as "9/11."

On 9/11, terrorists killed and injured thousands of people in the United States. The World Trade Center in New York City and a section of the Pentagon building in the Washington, D.C., area were destroyed by the airplanes.

Police officers, firefighters, doctors, and ordinary citizens joined together to rescue those harmed in the attacks. After 9/11, people across the United States cooperated to find new ways to protect America from future acts of terrorism.

Many people died in the 9/11 attacks. Why do you think the terrorists chose the World Trade Center as a target?

The Department of Homeland Security

President George W. Bush established the Department of Homeland Security after 9/11. The department helps organize other government agencies to prevent terrorist attacks and to respond when attacks occur.

Here are some of the changes that took place in the United States after the Department of Homeland Security was created:

- Airport security was improved.
- A national color-coded warning system was developed.
- People wanting to enter the United States had new rules to follow.

As a result of 9/11, airport security changed across America. What is shown in each of the photos below that makes flying safer for everyone?

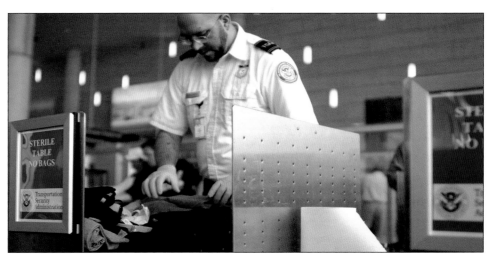

Wars in Iraq and Afghanistan

After the 9/11 attacks, the United States declared a "War on Terror." Many people in the United States believed the countries of Afghanistan and Iraq were allowing terrorists to live and train within their borders. Some people believed the leaders of Iraq were making powerful weapons to use in an attack on the United States or one of its *partners*.

Thousands of troops from the United States and other countries attacked Afghanistan and Iraq in the early years of the 21st century. Many people have died since the wars began, including people from New Hampshire. The wars in Afghanistan and Iraq continue today. Terrorism remains a serious problem throughout the world.

What Do You Think ?

Terrorism is not a new thing in the world. People in many countries have suffered from terrorist attacks for many years. Besides war, can you think of other ways for nations and organizations to handle problems and disagreements?

Afghan troops and a U.S. soldier participate in a training session in Afghanistan. What differences do you see in their uniforms? What kind of equipment do you see that helps the troops to fight terrorists?

Protecting Our Environment

Another *challenge* of the 21st century is to find new ways to protect the environment. Scientists have noticed that the atmosphere around Earth is getting warmer. As the atmosphere warms, Earth's climate changes. This change is causing glaciers to melt and sea levels to rise. Some plants and animals are not able to adapt to this change and are struggling to survive.

Scientists call this change *global warming*. Global warming is caused by pollution that comes from things like power plants, factories, and cars.

The Regional Greenhouse Gas Initiative (RGGI)

A power plant is a place that makes electricity. There are many power plants in the United States. A few are located in New Hampshire. Most power plants put large amounts of pollution into the environment.

In 2008, New Hampshire and nine other states began working on an agreement called the Regional Greenhouse Gas Initiative. The states work together to pass laws that limit the amount of pollution power plants pump into the air. This is one way our state is protecting the environment.

The State's First Wind Farm

If you drive near Lempster Mountain, you will see another way New Hampshire is working to help the environment. Twelve wind turbines have been placed at the top of the mountain. Each turbine is 256 feet tall and has three long blades. The blades spin when the wind blows. The spinning turbines use the power of the wind to make enough energy to send electricity to 10,000 homes each year. The wind farm is able to create energy without also producing pollution.

What Do You Think ?

Why do you think New Hampshire and other states believe it is important to cooperate with one another to lower pollution?

This wind turbine is used to make energy that supplies homes and businesses with electricity. What do you think the blades do?

Ken Burns, Documentary Filmmaker

One way we can protect our environment and create a more peaceful world is to learn how people handled problems in the past. Ken Burns is a documentary filmmaker in Walpole. He makes films that teach about historical events. Some of his films are about wars that took place long ago. Some of his films tell how people in the past worked to protect our environment.

Burns's most famous works include *The War, Lewis and Clark,* and *The National Parks: America's Best Idea.*

What Do You Think ?

New Hampshire is using new laws and new technologies to protect our environment. Can you think of other things we can do to stop global warming and keep our environment healthy?

This photo shows documentary filmmaker Ken Burns in his office in Walpole. What kinds of films do you think he likes to make?

LESSON 4 KEY IDEA REVIEW

1. Name three new technologies.
2. Why did the United States declare a "War on Terror"?
3. What is global warming?

Go to the Source

Astronaut from Our State

This is NASA Mission Specialist Richard Linnehan. He grew up in Lowell, Massachusetts, and Pelham, New Hampshire. The photo on the right shows him doing a spacewalk during the STS-123 mission. He is connected to the International Space Station's robot arm.

LOOK	THINK	DECIDE
Look at the left photo. How do you know he is an astronaut?	Look at the right photo. Do you think this looks like a fun job?	Why is it important for astronauts to travel into space?

Spotlighting Geography — Early Immigrants

The earliest immigrants to America settled in the 13 colonies. Later, immigrants continued to come to our state. Look at this globe that shows the countries from which immigrants of this period came. List the countries on a piece of paper. Next, use a map with a scale of miles to figure out about how many miles the immigrants had to travel from each of the countries to get to New Hampshire.

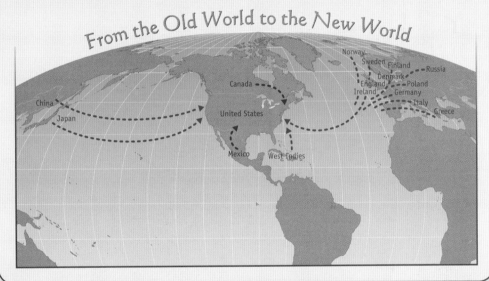

From the Old World to the New World

Becoming a Better Reader — Finding Details

Good readers know how to read to find details. Details support the main idea. If books only had main ideas, readers would be left with lots of questions. When reading a textbook or a nonfiction book, heads and subheads give clues about where to find the details. Write four details you learned about one of the main ideas from this chapter.

Reviewing the Big Idea

1. Describe two new inventions people used during the 20th century that we still use today.
2. What sacrifices did New Hampshire make to help World War I and World War II war efforts?
3. Why was women's suffrage significant in our history?
4. How did life during the Great Depression compare or contrast with life today?
5. How would life be different today if the Civil Rights Act was not created?
6. Explain, in your own words, what happened on September 11, 2001.

Big Idea

How does the government protect our rights?

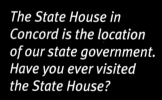

The State House in Concord is the location of our state government. Have you ever visited the State House?

Government for All of Us

Our government began with the idea that people have rights and freedoms. Today, people celebrate the freedoms of our country by voting, by learning how government works, and by participating in their communities.

Key Idea

What does "government by the people" mean?

Words to Understand

candidate
caucus
citizen
election
government
nominate
political party

Government in Our Lives

It takes the cooperation of many people to keep our communities running. We need water for our homes and businesses. We need sidewalks, streets, parks, schools, libraries, roads, and all sorts of other things. Our communities are able to provide the things we need because of the work of many people—especially people who work for our *government.*

Most of our national government is located in Washington, D.C. In 1808, Concord became our state capital. Most of our state government is located there. But government is not limited to these places. It is all around us. You, your classmates, and your family are important members of government, too.

This is the U.S. Capitol Building. This is where part of our national government is located. It is home to Congress and its two legislative bodies.

Our Government

Long ago, the first leaders of our country wrote an important document called the Constitution of the United States. It describes how our national government should work. Here are a few of the most important ideas in the U.S. Constitution:

- Government by the people
- Three branches of government
- Levels of government

Every state in the United States has its own state constitution. Our constitution took effect on June 2, 1784.

Government by the People

Citizens of the United States have the right to choose their government leaders. We do this by having *elections* in which people vote for leaders. If voters do not like what their leaders are doing, they can elect new leaders at the next election. In this way, citizens control the government's power.

This is a copy of our U.S. Constitution. There were two signers of the Constitution from New Hampshire: Nicholas Gilman and John Langdon. What are the first three words?

Voters use ballots like this one to cast their votes. Why do you think the ballot has to be "official"?

Political Parties

Political parties are groups of people who share the same ideas about government. Most people in the United States join either the Democratic Party or the Republican Party.

These are the two main political parties in New Hampshire and in the rest of the United States, but there are other parties, too. A **candidate** is a person who runs for government office. Political parties choose candidates and then work to get them elected. The parties raise money to pay for advertising, posters, flyers, and mailings. The candidates give speeches to try to win votes.

The elephant is the symbol for the Republicans.

The donkey is the symbol for the Democrats.

First in the Nation ✮✮✮✮✮✮✮

Selecting Presidential Candidates

Every four years, the people of the United States **nominate** candidates for president of the United States. Some states decide who they will nominate by holding caucuses. A **caucus** is a meeting in which people talk about their choices for president and then vote for the person they like best. Delegates from these states go to national conventions and nominate the candidates who won the most support during their caucuses.

Other states decide on their candidates by holding primary elections. A primary election allows citizens to vote for their favorite presidential candidates. Delegates from these states go to national conventions and nominate the candidates who received the most votes at their primary elections.

Illinois Senator and Democratic presidential hopeful Barack Obama addresses a crowd of people during a campaign rally at the Palace Theatre in Manchester. Read the sign in the photo. What do you think Senator Obama could be saying to the people?

CHANGE
WE CAN BELIEVE IN

The person who gets the most votes from delegates at a national convention is nominated as a political party's candidate for president of the United States. In 2008, the Democratic National Convention selected Senator Barack Obama as its candidate for president. The Republican National Convention selected Senator John McCain as its candidate for president. History was made on November 4, 2008, when Barack Obama became the first African American elected as our 44th president.

New Hampshire's First-in-the-Nation Primary

New Hampshire has held its presidential primary election before all other states since 1920. That is why New Hampshire's primary is called the "first-in-the-nation." In fact, state law requires the New Hampshire Secretary of State to hold the primary seven days before any other state.

Presidential candidates spend many months in New Hampshire before the state's primary election. They shake the hands of ordinary citizens. They answer people's questions. They give speeches asking voters to support them. The candidates know that everyone in the nation will watch to see who the people of New Hampshire vote for.

What Do You Think

Many people believe New Hampshire should not keep its first-in-the-nation status since the state's population does not represent the diversity of the rest of the United States. Other people believe our state's first-in-the-nation primary is an important tradition that should be continued. What do you think?

Dixville Notch

Dixville Notch has become famous because it holds the first presidential primary election, as well as presidential election, in the country. At midnight on primary day, every registered voter in town (about two dozen people) casts a vote for his or her favorite candidate. Workers immediately count the ballots and report the results to the rest of the nation. News crews from around the world travel to Dixville Notch to cover the first-in-the-nation primary results.

Dixville Notch is famous for being the first place in the country to hold primary and presidential elections. Who are the candidates being voted for in this picture?

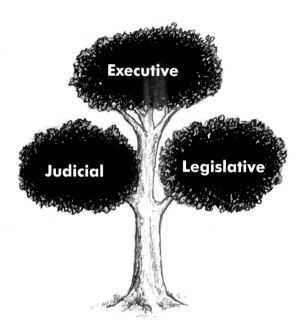

Branches of Government

The U.S. Constitution divides our government into three parts called branches. Each branch has the power to do only certain things. By dividing the government's power, no single branch can control the other two. The legislative branch makes laws. The executive branch carries out laws. The judicial branch explains what laws mean and decides punishments for people who break laws. Each branch checks the work of the other branches so power stays balanced between them.

Levels of Government

In the United States, we live under three levels of government. Local government makes decisions for people in towns, cities, and counties. State government makes decisions for everyone in our state. National government makes decisions for everyone in our country. Each level of government does different things. Look at the chart below to see what some of those things are.

LOCAL

PLACE: Towns, cities, counties
RESPONSIBILITIES:

Towns and cities: police and firefighters, schools, roads and bridges, water and sewer

Counties: records of births, deaths, marriages, property ownership; county courts

STATE

PLACE: New Hampshire
RESPONSIBILITIES: state lands and resources, state roads and bridges, driver licenses

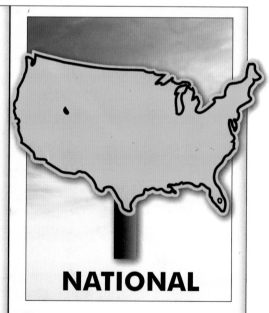

NATIONAL

PLACE: United States
RESPONSIBILITIES: national defense, printing of money, relations with other countries

Equal Representation

In our country, each person does not vote to make laws. Instead, voters cast votes for leaders called representatives. Some of our representatives travel to our national government in Washington, D.C. They vote to make laws that affect all of us.

Long ago, when the writers of the U.S. Constitution were creating it, they faced a difficult problem. Men from states with small populations wanted each state to have the same number of representatives. Men from states with large populations thought that was unfair. They thought they should have more representatives than states with fewer people.

To solve the problem, the writers decided that the legislative branch, called Congress, would have two parts. The two parts are the Senate and the House of Representatives.

Each state sends two senators to help make laws in the U.S. Senate. Each state also sends representatives to help make laws in the U.S. House of Representatives. The number of representatives is based on each state's population. For example, New Hampshire has two representatives because it has a low population. The least number any state can have is one representative.

At the Constitutional Convention, shown here, delegates decided that each state should have equal representation in one of two houses.

U.S. CONGRESS

Senate
100 senators
(two from each state)
Six-year term

House
435 representatives
(two from New
Hampshire)
Two-year term

New Hampshire, like all other states, sends two senators to represent us in the U.S. Senate. In the past, we sent two representatives to the U.S. House of Representatives. But this number changes when our population increases or decreases. To find out who our U.S. senators and representatives are, go to www.congress.org.

As a class, talk about questions you would like to ask your representatives. Is there something important you would like them to do for New Hampshire or for the nation? Write a letter or send an e-mail to your representatives.

New Hampshire Representative Jeanne Shaheen helps to create and pass laws for our state. What kind of law would you like her to make?

Our Responsibilities

A *citizen* is a person who belongs to a community. As citizens of the United States, we have responsibilities. We should respect the rights of others. We should obey laws our elected leaders have made. We should take part in government. This is what "government by the people" means. Voting is one way adults take part in government. You will have the right to vote when you turn 18.

There are other things you can do to be a good citizen. One of the first steps in being a good citizen is to learn how government works. You are doing that right now! You can also talk with your family about why rules and laws are important in your home and community.

LESSON ① KEY IDEA REVIEW

1. What are the two most common political parties?
2. What are the three branches of government?
3. What are the three levels of government?
4. How can you be a responsible citizen?

Our State Government

People in our state live by laws outlined in the U.S. Constitution and our state's constitution. Our state constitution sets up a state government made up of three branches: legislative, executive, and judicial.

State Legislative Branch

The state legislative branch is called the general court. It has a senate and a house of representatives. There are 24 state senators and 400 state representatives. New Hampshire has the largest state *legislature* in the nation.

Senators and representatives write and pass laws for our state. They are elected every two years. The members of the general court are not professional politicians. Most of them have other jobs or responsibilities. Some own businesses. Others are students. A few are homemakers. Many are doctors or lawyers.

Key Idea

Why do states need three branches of government?

Words to Understand

bill
jury
legislature
sponsor
testimony
veto

This is our state's legislative branch. What does it look like they are doing?

How a Bill Becomes a Law

The general court meets each year, beginning in January. During the session, senators and representatives study and vote on **bills** that people want made into laws. A bill is a written idea for a law. There may be as many as 1,000 bills for the legislature to consider each year!

1 Once a bill is drafted, the senator or representative *sponsoring* the bill presents it to the House or the Senate. The bill is given a number and read aloud and then it is sent to a committee.

2 At this stage of the process, sponsors get the opportunity to explain the bill, answer the questions of committee members, present supporting *testimony*, and hold public hearings. People who oppose the bill are also allowed to speak.

3 After committee members hear all the testimony, they make a recommendation to the rest of the House or Senate. Members of both the House and Senate can vote, "Do Pass," "Do Not Pass," or "Ought to Pass as Amended."

4 Members can now suggest changes or amendments to the bill. However, amendments are only adopted by a majority vote. Any adopted amendments must then be reviewed by committee members.

5 For a third time, the bill is read to members of the House or the Senate. Each group debates and votes on the bill. Once it has passed in the Senate or the House, it has to go through the same process in the other house. Bills must pass with a majority vote.

6 Once both the House and the Senate approve a bill, it heads to the governor for final approval. If the governor does not approve the bill, he will *veto* it. It will not become a law at that time.

VOTING BOARD

House Bill 22		
Representative	YES	NO
ADAMS	●	○
ANDERSON	○	●
BOYER	○	●
COLLINS	○	●
DAVIS	●	○
EDWARDS	○	●
FARMER	●	○
FRANKLIN	●	○
GAINES	○	●
GODDARD	●	●
HANSEN	○	●
HARRIS	○	●
HUGHES	●	●

7 If the bill is vetoed, there is still a way to make it a law. It goes back to the House where it began for another vote. If two-thirds of the legislators in both houses vote for it, it becomes law even if the governor is against it. This is one way the balance of power keeps any one group or person from making laws. It is an important part of our democratic government.

State Executive Branch

The governor of New Hampshire is required to have been an American citizen for at least 30 years and to have lived in our state for at least seven years.

"We are here to serve the people of New Hampshire. What they expect from us is results, or at least an honest effort to achieve them."

—*Jeanne Shaheen, New Hampshire's first woman governor*

This is the New Hampshire State House in Concord. It is home to our state's three branches of government. Can you name them?

Our state's executive branch is made up of a governor, executive councilors, and state agencies. Our governor is the head of the state executive branch. He or she works closely with an executive council. There are five councilors. Each one represents one-fifth of the state population. The members of the executive council represent different areas of our state. They approve how money is spent, confirm judges, and speak for the people of our state, as well as many more things. The governor and his or her council are elected every two years. Here are some of the responsibilities of the executive branch:

- Carry out state laws
- Suggest action for the legislature to take
- Sign bills into laws or veto them
- Appoint leaders of state agencies to oversee state parks, build and repair roads, and solve state problems in areas of health and education

State Judicial Branch

The judicial branch is the court system of our state. Courts settle arguments over the meanings of laws. They can also decide if a person is guilty of a crime.

What happens to a person who is charged with a crime? The person, along with his or her lawyer, goes to court. A judge, and often a *jury,* listens to the case. After everyone involved has been heard, the judge or jury decides if the person is guilty. If the person is found guilty of the crime, the judge decides what kind of punishment the person will get.

Some court cases do not involve crimes. Some people go to court because they feel they have been treated unfairly. For example, a person in an automobile accident might ask the court to decide who was to blame. The court will listen to everyone involved and decide what is fair.

The executive council approves the governor's choices for court judges. New Hampshire has four types of courts:

This photo shows the courthouse in Durham. What do you think people are doing inside of this building?

- **Supreme Court:** the highest court in New Hampshire; makes final decisions on laws and court cases in our state; made up of a chief justice and four associate justices

- **Superior Courts:** county-level courts; hear cases involving serious crimes, big lawsuits, property, and divorce

- **District Courts:** town- and city-level courts; hear cases involving smaller lawsuits and some criminal cases

- **Probate Courts:** decide issues related to wills, estates, and guardianship

LESSON ② KEY IDEA REVIEW

1. What are the responsibilities of the state legislative branch?
2. What are the responsibilities of the state executive branch?
3. What are the responsibilities of the state judicial branch?

What do our local governments do to help our communities be successful?

Words to Understand

alderman
board
community service
public service
selectman
volunteer

Our Local Governments

New Hampshire is divided into 10 counties and has more than 200 cities and towns. Each place in our state has different needs. Local governments help provide for those needs.

City and Town Governments

Cities and towns provide special services to their residents. Police officers, firefighters, community librarians, and public school teachers all work for cities and towns. Cities and towns pay for streets and schools. They pay for the park where you play ball and have picnics. If you play soccer on a city team, you are using a city service. If your city has a swimming pool, that is another city service.

People such as firefighters and police officers work for local governments. What do you think would happen if local governments did not provide these services?

Places like Manchester, Nashua, Portsmouth, and Concord are cities in our state. Cities are communities where thousands of people live and work.

Cities and towns have different forms of government, depending on how big they are. Some small towns elect leaders called **selectmen**. Many communities participate in annual town meetings. Some cities are governed by a mayor and a board of **aldermen**. Other cities are governed by a mayor and a city council. These people are elected by the citizens in their communities. They work together to make laws and rules that benefit their cities.

The photo above shows Nashua's governing body: Mayor Donnalee Lozeau (upper center) and the Board of Aldermen. They make the laws for the city. Why is it important for them to work together?

- Manchester has a mayor and a **board** of aldermen.
- Nashua has a mayor and a board of aldermen.
- Portsmouth has a mayor and a city council.
- Concord has a mayor and a city council.

Town Meetings

Each year, on the second Tuesday in March, voters in many New Hampshire towns gather to discuss and vote on things important to their communities. They ask questions like these: Should we raise taxes to build a new school? Should we buy a new snow plow truck or repair the old one? Should we hire another police officer? Each voter in the town has the right to stand up and give his or her opinion about the issues. After each person has had a chance to speak, everyone votes.

Town meetings have been important in New Hampshire since colonial times and will continue to be part of many communities. Growing populations have forced some towns and cities to stop holding town meetings. Instead, those communities use a representative form of government.

Taxes Pay for Services

New Hampshire's constitution gives our state, counties, cities, and towns the power to collect taxes. Tax money helps pay for services we use. Taxes are collected on land, homes, and buildings. Taxes are also collected when people eat in restaurants or stay in hotels. They are collected when people buy or sell property.

Taxes pay for construction and repair of roads. They pay for snow removal. They pay for libraries and public education. If you go to a public school, tax money pays for your building, your books, and your teachers' salaries.

How many *public services* can you find in this town?

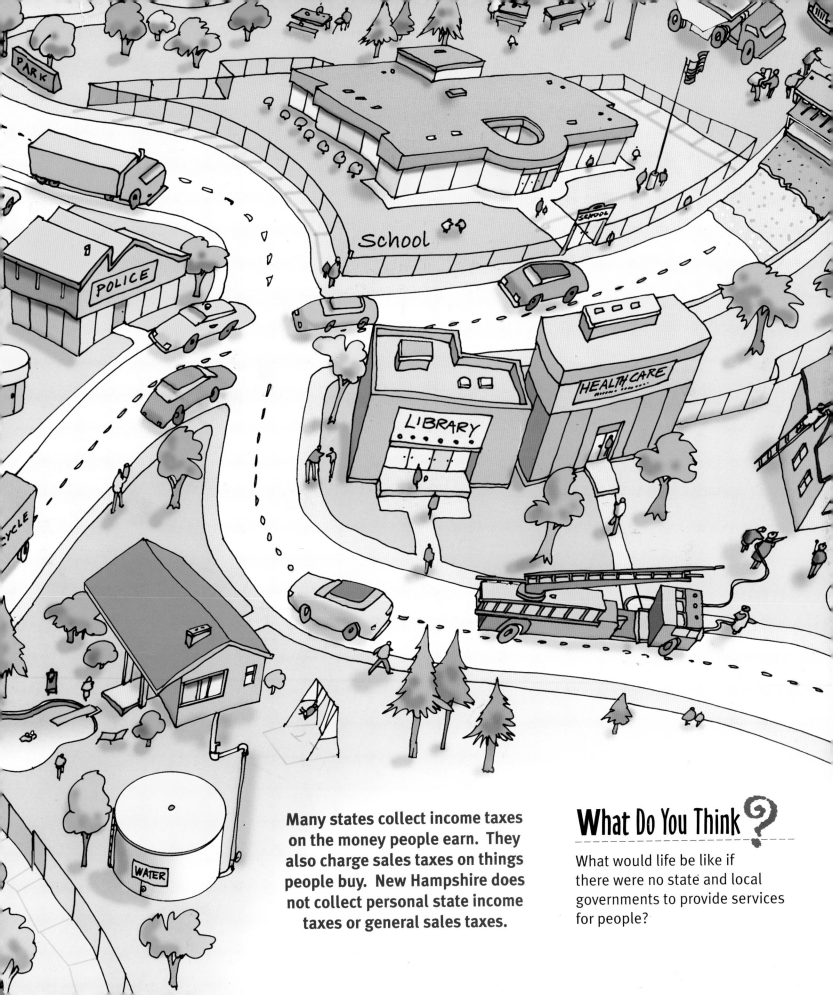

Many states collect income taxes on the money people earn. They also charge sales taxes on things people buy. New Hampshire does not collect personal state income taxes or general sales taxes.

What Do You Think?

What would life be like if there were no state and local governments to provide services for people?

County Governments

County governments use tax money to care for elderly and poor residents. They also operate courthouses and maintain jails. Can you find your county on the map?

This is downtown Nashua (left) and Laconia (below). They are county seats in our state. What county is Nashua in? What county is Laconia in? How do you know which cities are county seats on the map?

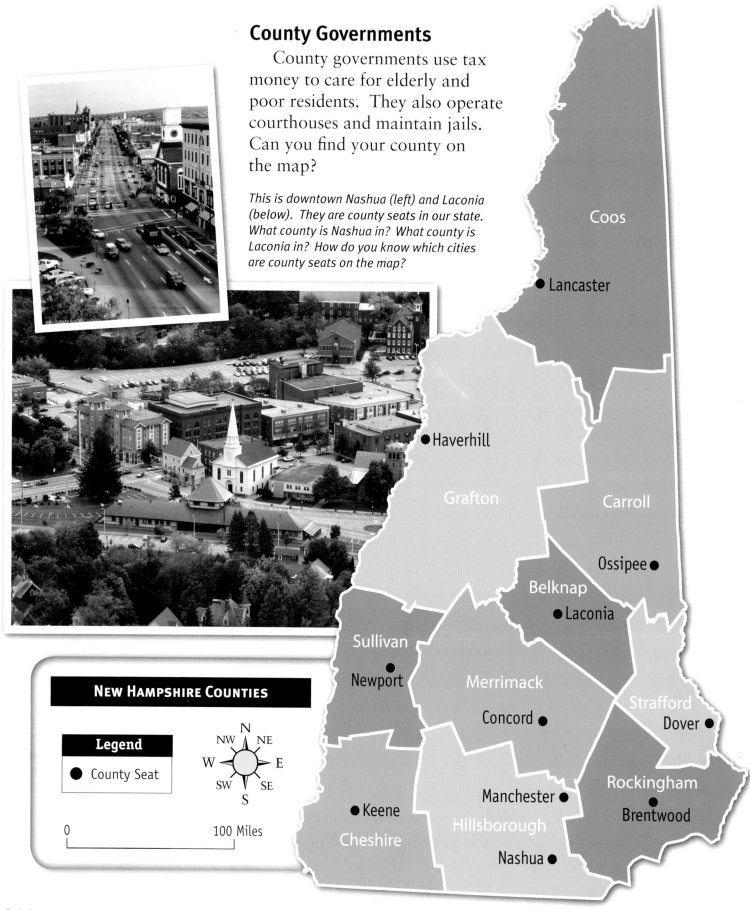

NEW HAMPSHIRE COUNTIES

Legend

● County Seat

N NE NW W E SW SE S

0   100 Miles

Coos

● Lancaster

● Haverhill

Grafton

Carroll

Ossipee ●

Belknap

● Laconia

Sullivan

● Newport

Merrimack

Concord ●

Strafford

Dover ●

● Keene

Cheshire

Hillsborough

Manchester ●

Rockingham

Brentwood ●

Nashua ●

Volunteering

New Hampshire is our home. The things that happen in our communities, businesses, governments, and environment depend on the choices we make as citizens. One way to be a good citizen in New Hampshire is to become a volunteer. *Volunteers* are people who help others without being paid for their time.

Many volunteers do community service. **Community service** is work you do to make your town or neighborhood a better place to live. The work can be as simple as picking up garbage on the side of the road or helping an elderly neighbor with chores around the house. You can also join an organization that does volunteer work in your community. The Girl Scouts and Boy Scouts are two examples of clubs that do volunteer work in communities.

This photo shows a Brownie Girl Scout in New Hampshire State Veterans Cemetery. What kind of community service is she doing?

LESSON ③ KEY IDEA REVIEW

1. What are some of the services provided in your town?
2. List three things taxes pay for.
3. How many counties does New Hampshire have?

Go to the Source

Liberty Bell Replica

This is a replica of the Liberty Bell. It sits on the front lawn of the State House in Concord. The U.S. Department of the Treasury had 55 replicas of the bell made—one for each state and U.S. territory, and one for Washington, D.C. Part of the inscription on the front reads: "Proclaim liberty throughout the land unto all the inhabitants thereof." After the Civil War, the original bell was a symbol of unity to people. It traveled throughout America encouraging freedom.

LOOK	THINK	DECIDE
What do you see on the front of the replica that looks out of place?	Why do you think there were so many replicas made of the bell?	Do you think the bell is a good symbol for freedom?

Spotlighting Geography | Our State Leaders

Who are New Hampshire's leaders today? Find out who represents your region or district. You could ask an adult, do research on the Internet, or look up the information under "State Government" in the blue pages of the phone book.

1. In which district do you live?
2. Who represents your district?
3. How far does this person have to travel to get to Concord, the New Hampshire state capital?

Reviewing the Big Idea

1. Can you name the three branches of government?
2. How do you benefit from the taxes people pay?
3. How is our state government similar to our national government?
4. Make a list of ways you can be a good citizen.
5. Describe in your own words how a bill becomes a law.
6. Where is the New Hampshire State House located?

Becoming a Better Reader | Compare and Contrast

Good readers often make comparisons to understand new information. Sometimes they will compare and contrast ideas or rank and order ideas to make comparisons. Use one of the comparison strategies you learned in this chapter to compare our national government to our state government.

Making a Living
in New Hampshire

*Have you heard of Stonyfield
Farm in Londonderry? Do
you know what they make?
What do you think this raw
processor is doing?*

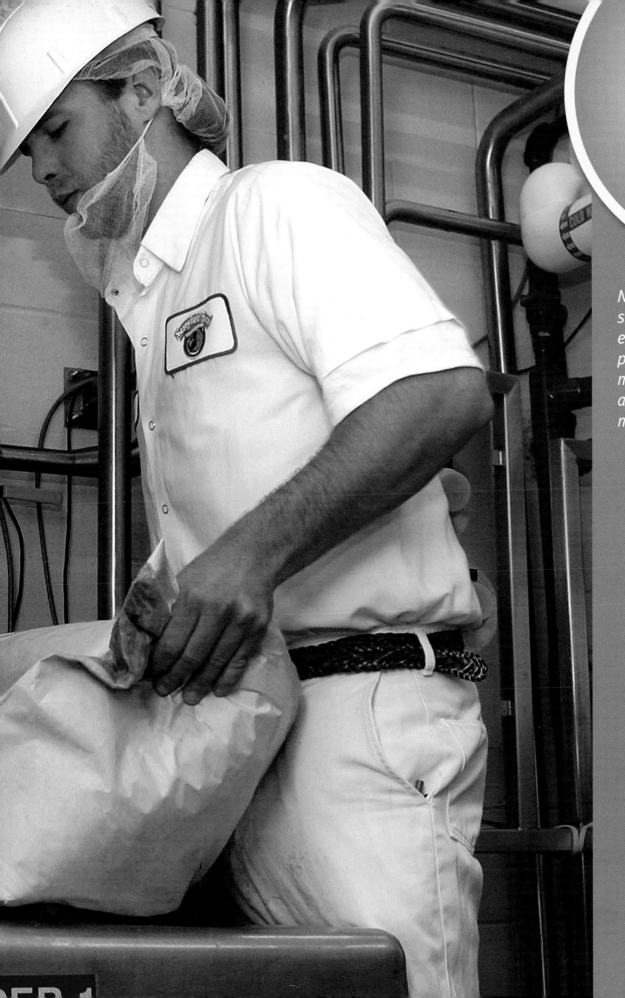

New Hampshire is a small state with a very strong economy. Our people, products, and services make money in our state and in thousands of markets around the world.

Key Idea

What is economics, and what types of economic systems exist in the world today?

Words to Understand

economics
employee
employer
entrepreneur
expense
free enterprise
good
market economy
producer
profit
recession
service

Our Economy

People have needs that they cannot go without. They need food, clothing, and shelter. People also have wants. They want things like cars, books, and bicycles. These are things that people would like to have but don't need to survive. Things like cars, books, food, and bicycles are called *goods*.

People also need things like health care and education. These are called *services*. Doctors, teachers, bankers, firefighters, and garbage collectors provide services. People who make goods or provide services are called *producers*.

Economics is the study of how people make money and spend it. It is also the study of how people get goods and services they need and want. In this chapter, we will learn how people in our state buy and sell goods and services.

People like doctors, dentists, and teachers provide services. What other jobs provide services?

Number from 1 to 10 on a sheet of paper. Read the list of jobs below. Write "G" next to the jobs that provide goods. Write "S" next to jobs that provide services.

1. Fixing a leaking pipe
2. Collecting the garbage
3. Teaching students
4. Making paint
5. Making engines for cars
6. Repairing cars
7. Delivering cheese to stores
8. Making telephones
9. Helping students check out library books
10. Checking people into hotel rooms

Economic Systems

Some countries have a command economy system. This means the government controls the system and owns the companies that produce goods.

The United States has a *free enterprise* economy. This means that in our country, people—not the government—own most of the companies. Anyone is free to start a business. A person who starts a business is called an *entrepreneur*.

Employers and Employees

A business owner or manager is the person who runs a company. He or she decides what to sell and what the price of a good or service will be.

Business owners often hire *employees* to work for them. Employees are paid for the hours and days they work or for the amount of work they do. The business owners who hire workers are called *employers*.

This employee works in a factory for an employer. What kind of factory do you think she works in?

Making a Living in New Hampshire

The Business Cycle

Our economy goes through good times and bad times. Sometimes there are plenty of jobs for people who want to work. Sometimes it is easy for people to earn money for things they want and need. These good times are called prosperity.

Other times there are not enough jobs for all of the people who want to work. During these times, it is hard for people to earn enough money to buy the things they need. These bad times are called *recession*.

These good times and bad times are part of the business cycle. Look at the chart to see how a business cycle works in our economy.

① Ten people want to buy cars. Seven cars are available.

② The price of cars goes up. People need more wages to buy cars. The cost of building cars goes up. The price of cars goes up.

③ When the price of cars is too high, fewer people want to buy cars.

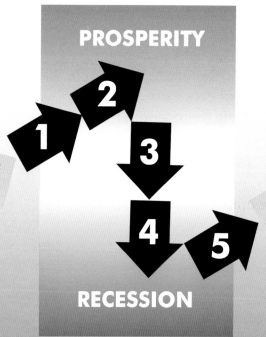

④ The car factory makes fewer cars. The car factory does not need as many workers. People have less money to spend. The economy slows down. The car seller lowers prices of the cars.

⑤ The cycle starts over.

Market Economy

A ***market economy*** connects people who want to sell things with people who want to buy things. We live in a market economy.

Our economy is made up of three parts: households, businesses, and government. Look at the chart to see how each of these parts connects to the others.

What kinds of things help our economy grow? How do you help our economy grow? Explain your answers.

MARKET ECONOMY

HOUSEHOLDS — BUSINESSES — GOVERNMENT

LABOR/PAYMENTS
INCOME/GOODS & SERVICES
SERVICES/INCOME
TAXES/LABOR
TAXES/GOODS & SERVICES
SERVICES/PAYMENTS

Activity | Be an Entrepreneur

Become a part of the free enterprise system in our country by thinking of what kind of business you would like to own. For example, if you like to play games, perhaps you would like to own a company that makes games. If you love chocolate, how about owning a chocolate factory? Or you can think of a business that your community needs, like a laundromat or a bakery.

After you have thought of a business, fill in the chart and answer the questions. Share your ideas with the class. Find out what kinds of businesses will make up your classroom's business community.

BUSINESS NAME:
GOODS FOR SALE:
NUMBER OF EMPLOYEES:
SUPPLIES NEEDED TO MAKE PRODUCT:

1. Why did you choose to own this type of business?
2. Where would you like your business to be located? Why?
3. How does your business help our state?
4. What kinds of things do you need to buy in order to run your business?
5. What would you like to do with the profit your company makes?

Factors of Production

Four things must work together before something can be sold as a good or a service. These things are called factors of production. The four factors of production are natural resources, capital resources, human resources, and entrepreneurs.

Study the drawing below to see all the steps and jobs required to build bicycles. Which job would you like to have?

Natural Resources

Natural resources are materials found in nature that companies can use to make products. A furniture company uses wood from trees to make chairs. A glass company uses sand to make windows.

Pretend you own a bicycle company. You use metal for bike frames and rubber for tires. You use electricity to run your machines.

Metal ore

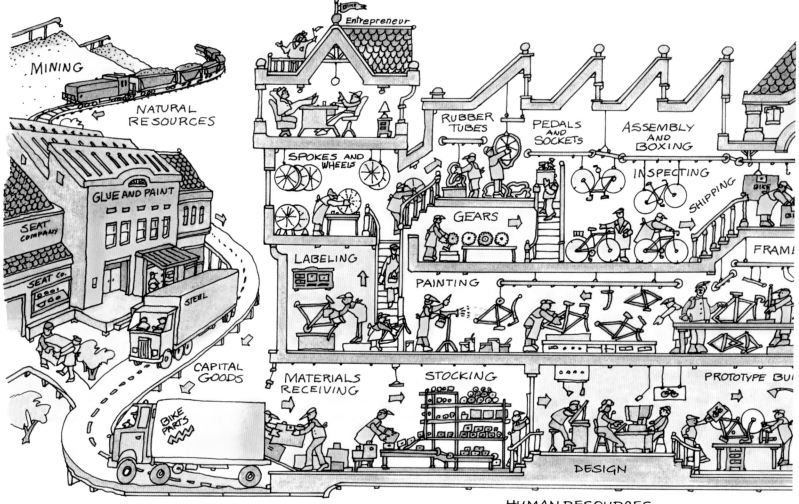

Capital Resources

You also need tools like screwdrivers, paint, and bike parts to make your bicycles. The money you spend to buy tools is called capital. When you use something you already have (like a screwdriver) to make something else (like a bike), you are using a capital resource.

Human Resources

To provide goods and services, people must work. Even if work is done by a machine, it takes people to build the machine and run it.

The people in your bicycle factory are your workers. They provide the work needed to make bikes. These workers are sometimes called human resources.

Entrepreneurs

An entrepreneur often begins his or her business with an idea or an invention. He or she must be willing to spend money to make the idea or business succeed.

By starting your own bicycle company, you are an entrepreneur. You use natural, capital, and human resources to make goods or to provide services.

What Do You Think ?

People have jobs as factory workers, teachers, farmers, pilots, dentists, and salespeople. What other kinds of jobs do people do in your community?

What would you add to these bikes to make people want to buy them? For example, you could add a horn or change the color. What do you think would create a demand for these bikes?

Making a Profit

Let's look at how your bicycle business earns money. You have to pay for the materials you use to make bikes. You have to pay employees to design, construct, and test your bicycles. These are your **expenses**. To make money, you must sell your bicycles for more than it costs to make them.

How do businesses determine the prices for their products? They look at three things:

- How much it costs to make the product
- Supply and demand
- Competition

How Much Does It Cost to Make It?

The first step in determining the price of a product is to figure out how much it costs to make it. Let's say it costs you $40 to buy the metal, plastic, and rubber and pay an employee to put one bike together. You will need to sell the bike for more than $40 to make a profit on it. **Profit** is the money the business has left after all expenses are paid.

Supply and Demand

The second step in determining the price of a product is to figure out how much people are willing to pay for it. The price will depend on how many bikes are made and how many people want one.

Imagine your factory makes 400 bicycles this year, but there are only 10 customers who buy them. You have a high supply and a low demand. You will probably need to sell the rest of the bikes at a lower price so more customers will buy them.

Now imagine your factory makes 20 bikes this year, but 50 customers want them. You have a low supply and a high demand. There is a limited number of bicycles because the supply is low. You will be able to sell the bikes at a higher price because so many people want them.

When products are limited, people have to make choices. Some might be willing to pay a lot of money for a bicycle. Others might choose to buy something else.

Businesses also have to make choices. If a company can't make enough bicycles to sell to everyone who wants to buy them (a high demand), then the company may choose to raise the price of each bike. If there are many bicycles available for sale (a large supply), a company may have to lower the price of each one to sell it.

Competition

The third step in determining the price of a product is to learn what other companies are doing. These other companies are your competition.

- Do other companies make similar bicycles? What do they charge? People often buy the products that cost the least.

- Can your company make a new type of bicycle or a better one? Can you offer buyers extra services that your competitors don't offer? For example, can you offer free repair services for one year?

Sometimes only one company makes a certain kind of product. If your company is the only one that makes bicycles, you could charge higher prices for bikes because you don't have any competition.

LESSON ① KEY IDEA REVIEW

1. What is economics?
2. What are the four factors of production?
3. How does a business determine the price for their products?

Key Idea

How do buyers affect the supply of goods and services?

Words to Understand

donate
generation
organic
recreation
specialization
tourism

Earning a Living in Our State

Long ago, almost everyone in our state worked on a farm, in a factory, or in the logging industry. Today, people in our state do many different kinds of jobs.

Some people have jobs that use special skills. People with a *specialization* do one type of job. They use their skills to help our economy produce more things. In a bike factory, some workers build the bike frames. Others test the bikes for safety. When each worker does his or her specialized job, the factory can produce many bicycles very quickly. What other types of work require specialization?

This person is welding a bicycle frame. Does this look like a job you would like to have?

Activity Where Do New Hampshire People Work?

Look at this bar graph to see some of our state's industries. Use the graph to answer these questions.

1. What are some of the jobs that are part of these industries? For example, teachers are part of the education industry.
2. Which industry employs the fewest people?
3. Which industry employs the most people?
4. How many people work for the government?
5. How many people work in natural resources and mining?
6. What industry employs almost 78,000 people?

1,200	NATURAL RESOURCES AND MINING
2,800	UTILITIES
12,100	INFORMATION
29,000	CONSTRUCTION
39,000	FINANCIAL ACTIVITIES
77,500	MANUFACTURING
95,800	GOVERNMENT
105,500	EDUCATION/HEALTH
147,500	WHOLESALE/RETAIL TRADE

(Source: NH Economic & Labor Market Information Bureau, 2008)

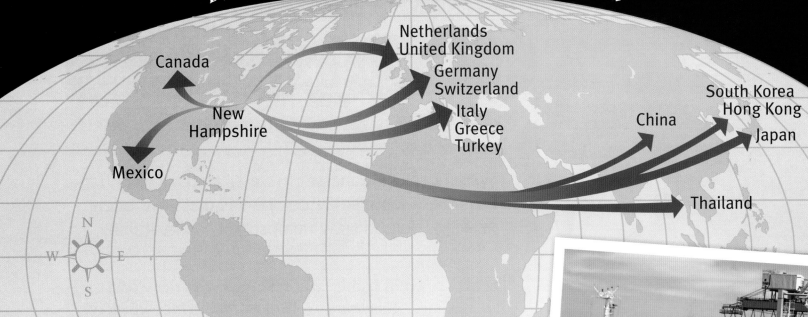

Canada

Netherlands
United Kingdom
Germany
Switzerland
Italy
Greece
Turkey

New Hampshire

Mexico

South Korea
Hong Kong
Japan

China

Thailand

N W E S

World Trade

New Hampshire plays an important role in world trade. Our roads, rivers, and airports link our state to other places around the globe. Transportation helps people import and export products. Many people make a living by selling their products and services all over the world.

New Hampshire's Exports

Most of our exports go to Canada, China, and Mexico. Exporting is a growing business in our state. New Hampshire exports nearly $3 billion worth of products to other countries each year. Take a look at this pie chart to see some of the goods New Hampshire companies export.

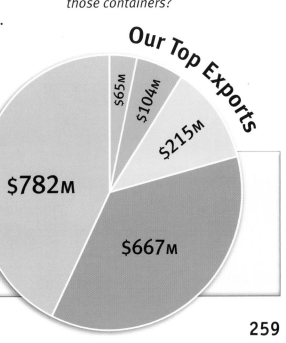

This is the Portsmouth Naval Shipyard. It is currently used as an area to repair nuclear-powered submarines. How do you think the workers at the shipyard move all those containers?

IRON AND STEEL

PLASTIC PRODUCTS

PHOTO EQUIPMENT & MEDICAL INSTRUMENTS

INDUSTRIAL MACHINERY

ELECTRICAL MACHINERY

(Source: NH International Trade Resource Center, August 2008)
(Based on U.S. Census Bureau, Foreign Trade Division statistics)

Our Top Exports

$65M
$104M
$215M
$782M
$667M

Making a Living in New Hampshire

New Hampshire PRODUCTS

New Hampshire businesses make all kinds of products. Let's read about some companies that have been making things in New Hampshire for a long time.

The tiny town of Dublin plays a big part in the world of magazines. It is home to **Yankee Magazine**, which is read by more than half a million Americans.

New Hampshire is famous for maple syrup. One of the best places to sample this popular treat is at **Fuller's Sugarhouse**. Fuller's has been family owned and operated for four **generations**. The company produces, packages, and sells maple syrup products in Lancaster.

Historic Peterborough is home to the **Peterboro Basket Company**. The company started almost 160 years ago when a man named Amzi Childs moved there from Massachusetts and began weaving beautiful baskets. Today, Peterboro Basket Company is a leader in the basket-making industry.

Stonyfield Farm in Londonderry has discovered a way to make and sell quality yogurt products while protecting the environment. The company was formed in Wilton in 1983 as an organic farming school. Today, Stonyfield Farm, the world's largest *organic* yogurt maker, recycles millions of pounds of materials each year and *donates,* or gives, money to organizations that help the environment. The company also donates millions of servings of yogurt to community events and local food banks.

The Freese family owns **Globe Manufacturing Company**. Globe has been designing and producing firefighting suits in Pittsfield since 1901. In fact, the company was the first to make and sell clothing that protected firefighters. Today, Globe Manufacturing Company is the largest and most trusted manufacturer of fire suits in the world.

What Do You Think?

Think of a New Hampshire business you know. Do you think any of the jobs in that business are examples of specialization? Explain your answer.

Which flavor of Blake's ice cream is your favorite? With over 40 flavors to choose from, it is not an easy decision! **Blake's Creamery** began producing and selling milk products in Manchester in 1900. It still sells dairy products and even runs several restaurants. Blake's uses milk and cream from local dairy farms in its products.

TOURISM

Tourism is one of our state's leading industries. Every year, millions of people from other states and countries visit New Hampshire. Most come during the summer and fall months. They come to enjoy our beaches, mountains, and fall leaves. They visit our museums, parks, restaurants, and hotels. They tour our historic towns and buildings. They attend our fairs and festivals. Tourists spend money on food, gas, hotels, and *recreation*. This helps businesses and workers in our state earn money. Look at the photos below and on the next page. How many activities have you done?

Portsmouth Harbor

Waterskiing in our state's many lake areas is a fun activity.

Camping is enjoyed by visitors to every region of our state.

The highest peak in our state, Mount Washington is a place where people enjoy hiking and camping.

Activities at or near our beaches are popular, such as fishing and taking a cruise.

Taking a train ride on the Conway Scenic Railroad is a great way for tourists to see some beautiful areas of New Hampshire.

Snow tubing

LESSON ② KEY IDEA REVIEW 🔑

1. What is specialization?
2. Describe one of New Hampshire's products.
3. How does tourism help our state earn money?

Making a Living in New Hampshire

LESSON ③ Spending and Saving

Key Idea

Why is it important to learn how to handle your money?

Words to Understand

budget
consumer
interest
opportunity cost
trade-off
value

What Is Money?

In colonial times, most people did business by bartering. They did not use money to buy and sell things. Instead, people traded skills and goods with one another. During the Industrial Revolution, using money became more common. People worked in factories and other businesses to earn money.

People in the United States once used pieces of gold and silver as money. Today, we use paper dollars and metal coins.

Bartering was the way most people got the goods they wanted in colonial times. What things do you see being traded in this illustration?

Compare the upper 10-cent note from 1863 with the lower 10-dollar bills from 1901 and 2004. What changes do you see?

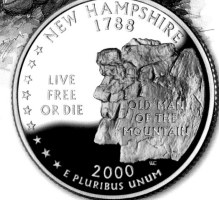

The United States Treasury began making new quarter designs for each state in 1999. What do the picture and words on our quarter say about New Hampshire?

Five Characteristics of Money

Most countries use paper bills and metal coins as money. But in some places around the world, things like beads, shells, cocoa beans, and salt are used as money! Anything can be used as money as long as it has these five characteristics:

- People must be able to carry it from place to place. Our paper bills and metal coins are lightweight and easy to carry.

- People must be able to separate it into parts. For example, a dollar bill is the same as four quarters.

- People must be able to use it over and over again for a long period of time. Most U.S. dollar bills are used by thousands of people and circulate for about two years before the U.S. Treasury replaces them.

- Everyone using it must agree it has *value*. Materials used to make U.S. money actually have little value, but we all agree to accept it in exchange for goods and services. That makes it valuable.

- It must be somewhat difficult to get. If everyone already has a lot of it, it decreases its value.

What Do You Think?

Imagine the United States has decided to stop using bills and coins as money. Can you think of something else we could use instead? Could we use beans or shells as money? Why or why not?

U.S. dollar bills are called paper money, but dollars are not made of paper. They are made of cloth. Workers at the U.S. mint blend cotton and linen to make money strong enough to survive many years of use. A mint is a place that prints money. It is against the law for any place except a mint to print money.

Spending Money

People are both producers and consumers. A **consumer** is a person who buys things. Anyone who spends money is a consumer. Most consumers want to spend their money wisely. They compare different brands and prices of products.

If you wanted to buy a new bike, how would you choose one? Bikes come in all styles, sizes, and colors. Some come with flashing lights or bells or water bottles. Comparing several bikes is an important part of choosing how to spend your money.

Do you want a road bike or a mountain bike? Do you want a green bike or a red one? When you have decided on the style and color of a bike, check several different stores to compare prices and features. After careful research, you will be able to choose a bike that fits your needs and wants, and has the best price.

This man is a consumer. What is he buying? Can you think of some other things he might need to buy at this store?

BRAND	PRICE	COLOR	EXTRAS
Brand A	$80	blue	bell
Brand B	$75	red	basket, bell, water bottle
Brand C	$100	silver	flashing lights, 10 speeds, water bottle

Trade-Offs

When you choose to buy one product instead of another, you make a trade-off. A **trade-off** is choosing not to buy one thing so you will have enough money to buy something else.

Imagine you have $10. You want to buy a book and a video game, but you don't have enough money for both. Which would you choose to buy? What trade-off would you make?

Adults have to make many trade-offs. They make **budgets**, or spending plans, to help them make decisions about what to buy.

You can also think of a trade-off as an **opportunity cost**. What opportunity is lost because of a person's choice? For example, imagine your school has land and money to build either a new gym or a new playground. The school decides to build a new gym. Using the land and money for a gym will cost your school the opportunity to build a new playground.

Checks and Cards

Do your parents have a checking account at a bank? After they put money into the account, they can write checks to pay for things. The money comes out of the checking account. Your parents can also use debit cards to pay for things. Debit cards subtract money from an account just like checks do.

Your parents might also use a credit card. Credit cards are a way to buy something now and pay for it later. Credit card companies lend your parents money to buy things. Your parents have to pay back at least some of the money each month. The companies also charge a fee each month for the service of lending money. This fee is called *interest*.

Saving and Planning

Some people do not save money. They spend all of their earnings as soon as they get paid. But it is important to save money for things you will need or want later. Suppose you get an allowance from your parents or earn money by walking dogs or mowing lawns. You earn $10 each week and want to buy a scooter that costs $100:

- How long will it take to earn the $100 if you save $10 each week?

- How long will it take if you save $5 each week and spend $5?

Banks are businesses that help people manage their money. Many people borrow money from banks so they can buy homes or cars. They also save their money in banks. If you save your money in a bank, the money does not simply remain in the bank. The bank lends the money to other people and businesses. It pays you a fee (interest) for allowing others to use your money.

LESSON ③ KEY IDEA REVIEW

1. Name one characteristic of money.
2. How are you a consumer?
3. Why is it important to save some of your money?

Go to the Source

The Shilling

When colonists arrived in America, they used money they were familiar with from England, such as pence, shillings, and pounds. Read what is printed on the one-shilling note below and answer the questions.

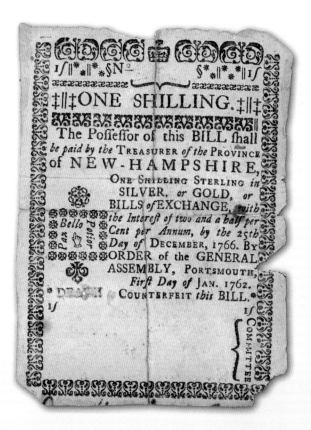

LOOK	THINK	DECIDE
Where was this shilling made?	Compare this shilling to a U.S. $1 bill. Which do you think is better to use? Why?	What would you add to this shilling to make it easy for people to know it is from our state?

CHAPTER REVIEW

Chapter 11

Spotlighting Geography — Geography and Business

List two businesses in New Hampshire that are part of each type of industry listed below. To find businesses, you could use this chapter, the Internet, or the yellow pages of the phone book.

Sales
Tourism
Technology
Health care

Choose one of the businesses you found. Describe how geography affects the business. You might think about things like the business's location, nearness to natural resources, and transportation options to transport goods to market.

Becoming a Better Reader — Draw Conclusions

You have become a better reader by learning new strategies for reading informational books. In this chapter, you learned to draw conclusions about what you read. Write about the most important thing you learned about New Hampshire. Be sure to include facts to tell about what you learned.

Reviewing the Big Idea

1. Can you explain why goods and services are important to our economy?
2. Provide an example of a market economy.
3. List three industries in New Hampshire.
4. How do exports help our economy?
5. How can learning about making, saving, and spending money help you in the future?
6. What are your thoughts on becoming an entrepreneur?

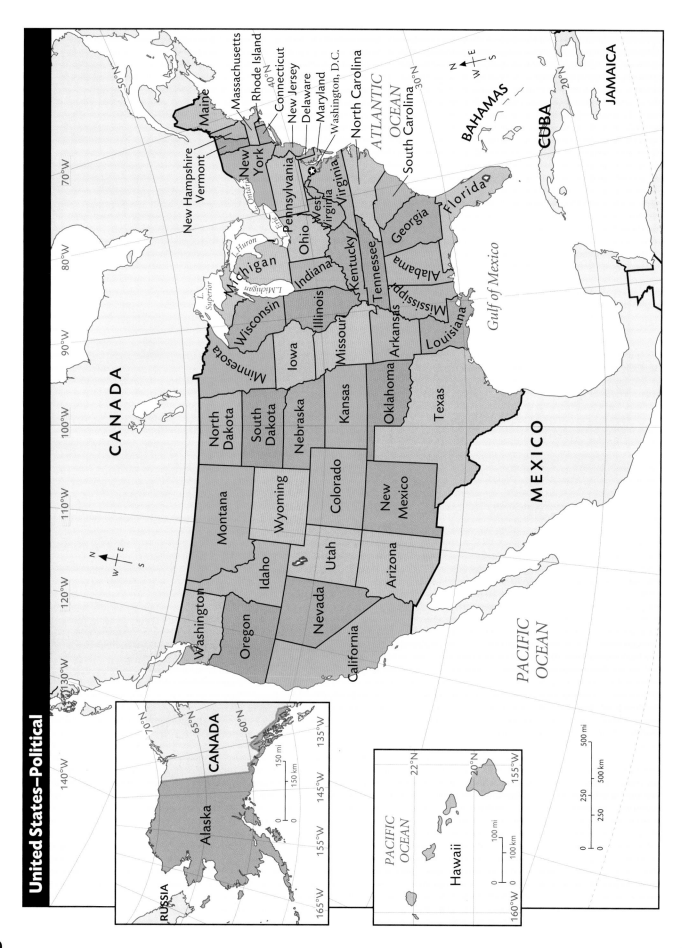

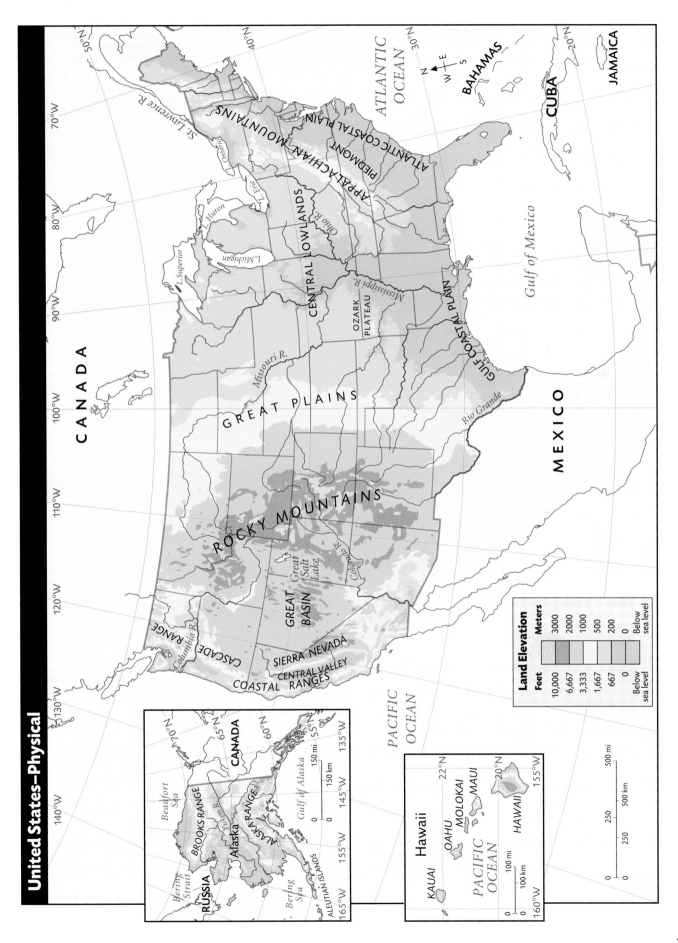

United States–Physical

CANADA

ATLANTIC OCEAN

BAHAMAS

CUBA

JAMAICA

St. Lawrence R.

L. Ontario

L. Erie

L. Huron

L. Michigan

L. Superior

APPALACHIAN MOUNTAINS

PIEDMONT

ATLANTIC COASTAL PLAIN

CENTRAL LOWLANDS

Ohio R.

Mississippi R.

OZARK PLATEAU

GULF COASTAL PLAIN

Gulf of Mexico

Missouri R.

GREAT PLAINS

Rio Grande

MEXICO

ROCKY MOUNTAINS

Great Salt Lake

Colorado R.

GREAT BASIN

Columbia R.

CASCADE RANGE

SIERRA NEVADA

CENTRAL VALLEY

COASTAL RANGES

PACIFIC OCEAN

Land Elevation

Feet	Meters	
10,000	3000	
6,667	2000	
3,333	1000	
1,667	500	
667	200	
0	0	
Below sea level	Below sea level	

500 mi

250

0

500 km

250

0

CANADA

RUSSIA

Beaufort Sea

BROOKS RANGE

Yukon R.

Alaska

ALASKA RANGE

Gulf of Alaska

Bering Strait

Bering Sea

ALEUTIAN ISLANDS

150 mi

150 km

0

0

70°N

65°N

60°N

55°N

135°W

145°W

155°W

165°W

Hawaii

KAUAI

OAHU

MOLOKAI

MAUI

HAWAII

PACIFIC OCEAN

22°N

20°N

155°W

160°W

100 mi

100 km

0

0

Atlas

New Hampshire–Political

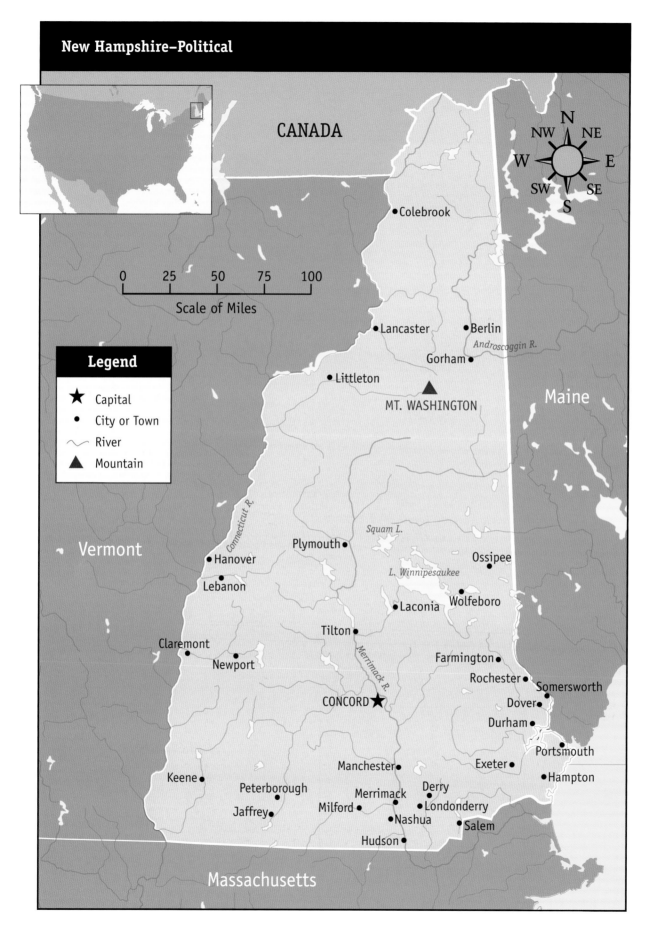

CANADA

• Colebrook

Scale of Miles
0   25   50   75   100

Legend
★ Capital
• City or Town
〜 River
▲ Mountain

• Lancaster   • Berlin
                Androscoggin R.
           Gorham •

• Littleton

▲
MT. WASHINGTON

Maine

Vermont

Connecticut R.

Squam L.

Plymouth •

Ossipee •

• Hanover

L. Winnipesaukee

• Lebanon

Laconia •   Wolfeboro •

Tilton •

Claremont •

Farmington •

• Newport

Rochester •
          Somersworth •

CONCORD ★

Merrimack R.

Dover •
Durham •

Portsmouth •

Manchester •

Exeter •
          • Hampton

Keene •

Derry •

Peterborough •

Merrimack •
          Londonderry •

Jaffrey •

Milford •

Salem •

Nashua •

Hudson •

Massachusetts

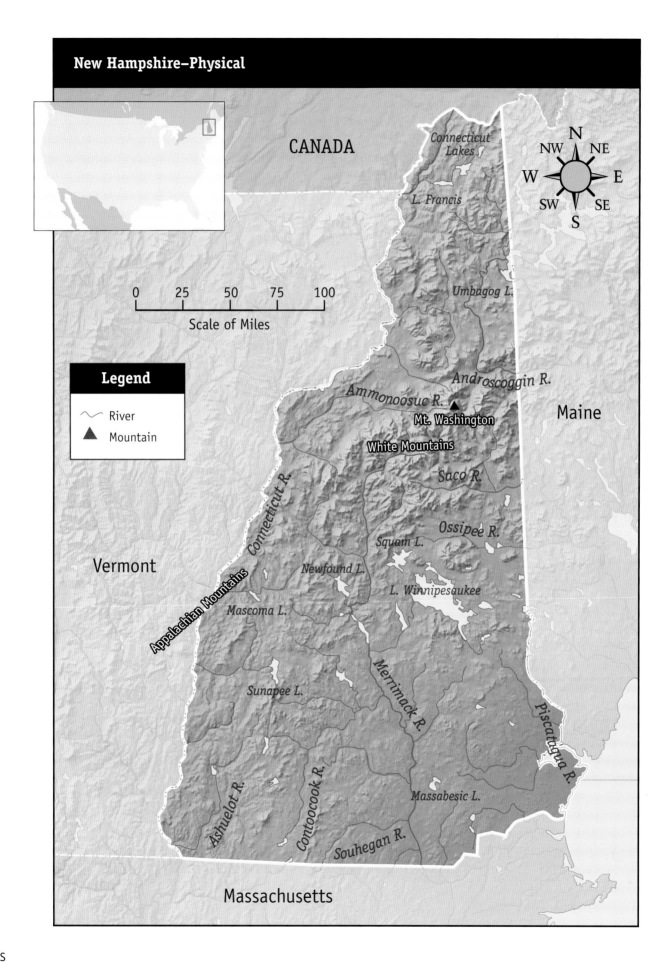

CANADA

Connecticut Lakes

L. Francis

Umbagog L.

N
NW · NE
W · E
SW · SE
S

Androscoggin R.

Ammonoosue R.

▲ Mt. Washington

White Mountains

Saco R.

Maine

0   25   50   75   100
Scale of Miles

Legend

∿ River
▲ Mountain

Ossipee R.

Squam L.

Connecticut R.

Newfound L.

Vermont

L. Winnipesaukee

Appalachian Mountains

Mascoma L.

Merrimack R.

Sunapee L.

Piscataqua R.

Ashuelot R.

Contoocook R.

Massabesic L.

Souhegan R.

Massachusetts

Atlas

Glossary

The definitions listed here are for the **Words to Understand** as they are used in this textbook.

A

abolish: to do away with something
abolitionist: a person who wanted to end slavery
absolute location: the exact spot where a place can be found
adapt: to change over time in order to survive
agriculture: the business of raising crops and animals to sell
alderman: a city leader
amend: to change
amendment: a change or addition to a constitution
ancestor: a relative who lived before
apprentice: a person who learns a trade from a skilled worker
archaeologist: a scientist who learns about ancient people by studying the things they left behind
architecture: the design of a building
artifact: something people made or used in the past and left behind
assassinate: to murder by sudden attack

B

barter: to trade
bill: a written idea for a law
blacksmith: a person who makes tools from iron
board: an official group of persons who guide and manage activities of other groups
bog: a wet area of land with trees or shrubs
branch: one part of government (executive, legislative, judicial)
breechcloth: a piece of animal skin tied around the hips and thighs, worn by Native Americans
budget: a spending plan

C

cable: a strong, metal rope that carries electricity
candidate: a person who runs for government office
caption: an explanation of a picture or illustration
captive: a prisoner
capture: to catch
cardinal direction: one of the four main directions on a compass (north, south, east, west)
cargo: goods that are being transported
caucus: a meeting in which people talk about their choices for a government office and then vote for the person they like the best
cause: a reason or motive for doing something
celebration: a joyful event held to honor something or someone
century: 100 years
ceremony: a special gathering
challenge: a call to a special effort
citizen: a person who belongs to a community
civil rights: the freedoms and powers people have as members of communities, states, or nations
climate: the weather of a place over a long period of time
coach: a large carriage pulled by horses
cog: a gear fitted into a slot in a gearwheel
colony: a settlement under the control of a country far away

communication: the exchange of information between people
community service: work done to make a town or neighborhood a better place to live
condition: surrounding
congress: a group of representatives who work out problems and make laws
constitution: a document that describes how a government is organized
consumer: a person who buys things
continent: a large land area
convert: to change a person's religion or beliefs
cooperation: working together
council: a group of people who meet to discuss important things and make decisions
culture: the way a group of people live

D-E

debate: an argument
decade: 10 years
declaration: an announcement that tells people about an important decision
declare: to announce officially
descendant: one's child, grandchild, great grandchild, and so on
determine: to decide
discovery: to find and learn about something new
document: a paper that contains information
donate: to give
economics: the study of how people make money and spend it
economy: the way people use their resources to make, sell, buy, and use goods and services
ecosystem: a community of plants and animals that depend on each other to live
election: the process of voting people into office
elevation: how high a place is above the level of the ocean
emancipation: freedom or release from slavery
emblem: a design or symbol that represents something
employee: a person who works for someone else
employer: a person who owns or runs a company
entitle: given a right to
entrepreneur: a person who starts a business
equator: the imaginary line that circles the middle of the globe (0 degrees latitude)
establish: to start or organize something
evidence: proof
executive: the branch of the government that carries out the laws
expense: money spent to make a good or provide a service
explorer: a person who travels unknown areas to find new things or to answer questions
export: to send goods somewhere

F

fact: something that is true and can be proven
famine: a time when there is not enough food for everyone

fast: to not eat
fife: a flute
flax: a long, thin plant
foliage: leaves
foreman: a person in charge of a logging operation
framework: a frame built with parts that are fitted and joined together
free enterprise: a type of economy in which the people own most of the companies
frontier: the edge of unsettled territory; wilderness

G-H

generation: a group of people born and living at about the same time
geography: the study of Earth's land, water, people, and other living things
glacier: a large, slow-moving sheet of ice
global warming: the warming of Earth's temperatures that causes changes to climates and environments
good: something that is made, bought, and sold
government: the system by which cities, states, or nations are ruled
grant: land or money that is given for free
harbor: a sheltered part of the ocean that is deep enough for ships to sail into
harpsichord: a keyboard instrument
hemisphere: half of Earth
herb: a plant used for food or medicine
history: the record of the past
Holocaust, human feature: something made by people, such as cities, homes, bridges, and roads
humid: moist

I-L

illegal: against the law
image: a picture
immune: to be able to resist disease
import: to bring goods in from somewhere
indenture: to bind a person to service with a formal contract
independent: not ruled by anything or anyone else
industry: a field of business, such as shipbuilding, lumbering, tourism, and so on
inspect: to look at closely
interest: the fee charged for borrowing money; the fee paid to a person for putting money into a bank
intermediate direction: a direction in between the four main directions on a compass (northeast, northwest, southeast, southwest)
Internet: worldwide system of connected computers
invention: a new product, service, or idea created by someone
judicial: the branch of government that enforces the laws
jury: a group of people who listens to a court case and decides if a person is guilty
latitude: an imaginary line that circles Earth running north and south
launch: to start
legend: a story that explains history or why things are the way they are
legislative: the branch of government that makes the laws

legislature: a group of elected people who have the power to make laws
longhouse: a Native American home that was long, rectangular, and made of cedar logs
longitude: an imaginary line that circles Earth running east and west
lowland: land that is low in comparison to the surrounding land
Loyalist: a person during the American Revolution who did not want to break away from Britain

M

manufacture: to make something by hand or with a machine
market economy: an economy that connects people who want to sell things with people who want to buy things
marsh: an area of low, wet land
massacre: the violent killing of lots of people at one time
memorial: something that reminds people of a person or an important event
merchant: a person who buys and sells things or runs a store
migrate: to move from one place and settle in another
militia: a small, local army
moccasin: a shoe made from moose fur and leather, worn by Native Americans
monument: something built to honor the memory of a person or an event
moral: the meaning of a story
motto: a saying that expresses the purpose of a person or organization

N

natural resource: something found in nature that people use
network: a system of people or buildings related to one another in some way
neutral: not choosing one side or the other
nomad: a person who travels from place to place, searching for food
nominate: to choose a candidate
nonrenewable: unable to be reused or replaced
notch: a V-shaped canyon formed by glaciers

O-P

obstacle: something that stops progress
official: having approval
opinion: something someone thinks or believes
opportunity cost: gaining something at the cost of giving up something else
opportunity: a chance to do something
oral history: history told aloud and passed from person to person
organic: natural
partner: a person or group who shares in an action or goal
patent: a paper that gives an inventor the sole right to make and earn money from his or her invention
Patriot: a person during the American Revolution who wanted independence from Britain
permanent: lasting a long time
petition: to request something from the government in writing
physical feature: something made by nature, such as soil, lakes, plants, animals, and climate

plantation: a large farm

point of view: the way a person thinks about something that happened

political party: a group of people who share the same ideas about government

population: the number of people who live in a place

portrait: a description of a person

prehistoric: before history

preserve: to keep safe from harm or change

primary source: something made, written, or used by people who were at an event when it occurred

prime meridian: the imaginary line that divides Earth equally into eastern and western hemispheres (0 degrees longitude)

producer: a person who makes goods or provides services

product: something that is made, bought, and sold

profit: the money a business has left after all expenses are paid

prosperity: wealth

public service: a service given for free to the public.

Q-R

quarry: a place where rock is taken out of the ground

quill: a feather used for writing

raid: to attack

ransom: to deliver a person from captivity in exchange for money or goods

ratify: to approve

ration: to buy in limited amounts

rebel: to go against someone or something

recession: a time when the economy is bad and it is hard for people to earn enough money to buy the things they need

Reconstruction: the rebuilding of the nation after the Civil War

recreation: entertainment or a hobby that gives enjoyment

regiment: a large group of soldiers

region: an area of land that shares common features

relative location: where a place is in relation to other places or things

renewable: something that will come back or can be used over and over again

replica: a copy of something

represent: to stand or act in the place of something

representative: a person elected to speak, act, or vote for other people

resident: a person who lives in a place

resign: to give up a position or job

retreat: to withdraw or move back

revenge: the act of getting back at someone for something they did wrong

revival: a renewed interest in something

revolution: a time when people fight to replace one government with a different government

S

sachem: a Native American leader

sacrifice: to go without things a person wants or needs

sapling: a young tree

satellite: a machine in space that orbits the Earth, sun, moon, and so on

sawmill: a place where logs are cut into lumber

seal: a symbol used on documents, flags, and so on

seaport: a city or town by the ocean where ships load and unload cargo

secede: to leave one country to form another

secondary source: something written, said, or made by someone who was not there at the time of an event

selectman: a town leader

service: work done for a person for money

shaman: a person who Native Americans believed could communicate with the spirit world and heal the sick

shanty: a temporary home

sinew: a tendon

situation: position

slave: a person who is owned by another person and forced to work without pay or freedom

social: having to do with relationships with other people

specialization: using skills to provide a specific service or make a specific product

sponsor: to promise or answer for

strike: to refuse to work until certain conditions are met

stock: (Chapter 8) the wooden piece of a gun where the barrel is attached. (Chapter 9) a small piece of a company

suffragist: a person who fought for women's right to vote

surrender: to give up

symbol: something that stands for something else

T

tavern: a place where colonial people met to eat, drink, and talk

tax: money people must pay to a government

technology: the science of improving tools, machinery, and electronics

terrorist: a person who uses violence or threats to make people do what the terrorist wants

testimony: a statement given in support of something

textile: fabric

timeline: a line that shows the order events happened

tourism: the industry of making money from people who visit

trade-off: choosing to not buy one thing so you will have enough money to buy something else

tradition: a way of life handed down from parents to children

transportation: moving from place to place

treason: going against the government

treaty: a written agreement

tribe: a group of Native Americans

U-W

unalienable: unable to be taken away

Underground Railroad: a system of routes and safe houses used to help slaves escape

upland: land that sits higher than other land

value: the worth of something

veto: to reject a bill

vision quest: a Native American ceremony in which boys were to find their guardian spirits

volunteer: a person who helps others without being paid for his or her time

war bond: a paper, which people bought from the government to raise money for a war, that could be traded in later for more money

waterway: a body of water, such as a river, used for traveling or shipping.

weather: temperature, wind, rain, or snow happening at a certain time

weir: a fence built across a stream used to trap fish

wetland: a low area of land that is covered by water long enough for plants to grow

wigwam: a Native American home that was oval shaped and covered with bark or hides

Index

Credits

The following abbreviations were used for sources from which several images were obtained:

AP Images – Associated Press
Granger – The Granger Collection, New York
GSP Archives – Gibbs Smith, Publisher Archives
iStock – iStockPhoto.com
Jupiter – Jupiter Images
LOC – Library of Congress Prints and Photographs Division
NHHS – New Hampshire Historical Society
NWPA – North Wind Picture Archives
SS – ShutterStock.com

All other maps, photos, or illustrations are public domain, royalty free, or from the Gibbs Smith, Publisher Archives.

Chapter One: 2-3 Lee Snider/Photo Images/Corbis; 4 (t) Jorg Jahn/SS, (tr) Jupiter, (lc) Jupiter, (bl) Jupiter, (br) Piotr Sikora/SS; 5 NHHS; 7 (c) Dallas Museum of Art, (r) Gelpi/SS; 8 GSP Archives/ Shauna Kawasaki; 9 Jupiter; 10 (c) LOC, (b)GSP Archives/Janis J. Hansen; 11 (t) Jupiter, (b) Stephen Bicknell/Hudson Museum; 12 (t) LOC, (b) Jupiter; 13 (t) Ken Canning/SS, (b) Lora Clark/SS; 14 (t) Tim Pleasant/SS, (b) Strawberry Banke; 15 (r) Ferenc Szelepcsenyi/SS, (c) Kelpfish/SS, (l) prism68/SS; 16 NHHS; 18 (tl) John A. Anderson/SS, (bl) Alexander Chelmodeev/SS, (cr) rebvt/ SS, (br) not available/SS; 19 (tl) not available/SS, (tr) Mike Rogal/ SS, (c) Morozova Tatyana Manamana/SS (bl) SS; 20 (bl) Jupiter, (br) Beth Rexford; 21 (t) PJ Fischer Photography (b) Erik Freeland/Corbis; 22 NHHS; 23 iofoto/SS.

Chapter Two: 24-25 NASA; 27 (t) George Spade/SS, (b) LOC; 31 Stephen VanHorn/SS; 32 Andrea LG Ferguson/SS; 33 Nicholas Peter Gavin Davies/SS, (inset) Jupiter; 34 Robert Manley/SS; 35 (t) g.lancia/SS, (b) Jim Cole/AP Images; 36 (l) maggie/SS, (r) Carl Southerland/SS; 37 (l) rebvt/SS, (r) Chee-Onn Leong/SS; 38 Danis Derics/SS; 39 (left to right) Natalia Bratslavsky/SS, not available/ SS, Laurin Rinder/SS, Eric Patterson/SS; 41 (l) Laurence Gough/ SS, (r) Steve Broer/SS; (l) Swenson Granite Works, (r) Robert Manley/SS; 43 (l) Chee-Onn Leong/SS, (r) Andrea LG Ferguson/ SS; 44 (bkgrd) Lawerence M. Yerxa, Mount Washington Observatory; 45(t) Bonnie J. Anderson/SS, (b) Wayne Johnson/SS; 46 (l) not available/SS, (r) Gila R. Todd/SS; 47 (l) Scott David Patterson/ SS, (r) Martine Oger/SS; 48 ShutterVision/SS; 49 Denis Vrublevski/SS; 50 Steve Broer/SS; 51 World Wide Photos, AP.

Chapter Three: 54-55 North Wind Picture Archives; 57 (t) GSP Archives/Neal Anderson, (b) Michael Bagdon/SS; 58 (t) Jupiter, (b) GSP Archives; 60-61 NHHS; 62 GSP Archives, 63 (t) Tara Prindle, (b) GSP Archives/Gary Rasmussen; 64 (t) Jupiter, (r) LOC; 65 (t) Utah Museum of Natural History, (b) Kindra Clineff; 66 (t) Perry Correl/SS, (bl) Minnesota Historical Society/Reed St. Paul, (br) Canadian Museum of Civilization; 67 Courtesy of the Abbe Museum, Bar Harbor, Maine, Photo by Stephen Bicknell; 68

LOC; 69 Martin Pate Art; 70-71 GSP Archives/Gary Rasmussen; 72 NWPA; 73 (t) Jupiter, (b) World Wide Photos, AP/Toby Talbot, Staff; 74 Peabody Essex Museum.

Chapter Four: 76–77 NWPA; 78 GSP Archives/Neal Anderson; 79 Jupiter; 80 (l) Jupiter, (c) NWPA; 81 Granger; 82 Blue Lantern Studio/Corbis; 83 (bkgrd) Michael Rubin/SS, (inset) GSP Archives; 84 NHHS; 85 Granger; 86 Jupiter; 87 Granger; 88-89 (bkgd) C Salisbury/SS, (r) Bettmann/Corbis; 90-91 (bkgd) Charles Knox/SS, GSP Archives; 91 (c) NWPA, (r) GSP Archives; 92 NWPA; 93 NWPA; 94 Woodman Institute Museum; 95 (t) Jupiter, (b) James Randklev/Corbis; 96 GSP Archives/Janis J. Hansen; 97 (t) LOC, (b) GSP Archives/Neal Anderson; 98 Courtesy of the Trustees of the Haverhill Public Library, Special Collections Department; 99 bluehill/SS.

Chapter Five: 100-101 NHHS; 102 (r) LOC, (b) NWPA; 103 (cl) Jupiter, (c) Jupiter, (inset) Courtesy Henniker, NH Historical Society Collection; 104 Jupiter; 105 (t) Private Collection, © Michael Graham-Stewart/The Bridgeman Art Library International, (b) Granger; 106 (l) Courtesy Strawbery Banke Museum/ John Dunkle, (r) ©Ralph Morang/Courtesy Strawbery Banke Museum; 107 Lee Snider/Photo Images/Corbis; 108 NHHS; 109 NWPA; 110-111 GSP Archives/Gary Rasmussen; 112 (t) Granger, (b) GSP Archives/Neal Anderson; 113 GSP Archives/Neal Anderson; 114 (c) NWPA, (l) GSP Archives/Janis J. Hansen; 115 (t) GSP Archives/Neal Anderson, (bl)Jupiter, (bc) GSP Archives/Michelle Pierce; 116 Richard T. Nowitz/Corbis; 117 (t) LOC, (b) NHHS; 118 (t) Smithsonian Institute, (r) Jupiter, (b) Jupiter; 119 (t) LOC, (b) Jupiter; 120 (t) NHHS, (b) Jupiter; 121 Colonial Williamsburg Foundation; 122 New York Public Library; 123 (t) LOC, (b) Lee Snider/Photo Images/Corbis; 124-125 (bkgrd) idiz/SS, 125 GSP Archives/Neal Anderson; 126 Dallas Museum of Art; 127 Gelpi/ SS.

Chapter Six: 128-129 SuperStock; 130-131GSP Archives; 132 Bettmann/Corbis; 133 LOC; 134 (t) The British Library, (b) GSP Archives/Janis J. Hansen; 135 NWPA; 136 Granger; 137 LOC; 138 (t) LOC, (b) Jupiter; 139 (t) LOC, (b) Bettmann/Corbis; 140-141 NHHS; 142 Courtesy of the Jaffrey Public Library; 143-145 LOC; 146 United States Capitol Historical Society; 147 Stephen Coburn/SS; 148-149 GSP Archives/Jim Hunt; 150 LOC.

Chapter Seven: 152-154 NHHS; 155-159 LOC; 160-161 GSP Archives/Neal Anderson; 162 (bkgrd) Adrian Cheah/SS, (inset) not available/SS; 163 Jim Lozouski/SS; 164 (t) Photo courtesy of the Cole Land Transportation Museum, Bangor, ME, (b) NHHS; 165 (l) Donald R. Swartz/SS, (r) Thomas W. Nesbitt/SS, (b) NHHS; 166 (l) LOC, (c) NHHS, (r) Courtesy Mount Washington Resort; 167 Bettmann/Corbis; 168-169 GSP Archives/Neal Anderson; 170-171 LOC; 172 (t) Jupiter, (r) LOC; 173 Jupiter; 174 LOC.

Chapter Eight: 176-177 National Park Service; 178 LOC; 179 (b) Corbis, (inset) LOC; 180 Granger; 181 GSP Archives; 182 The

Art Archive/Corbis; 183 LOC; 184 (t) LOC, (b) NHHS; 185 NHHS; 186-193 LOC; 194 Machias Savings Bank/Robert E. Goodier Collection; 195 (t) Beth Van Trees/SS, (b) LOC; 196 (t) NYPL; 197 NWPA.

Chapter Nine: 200-201 SuperStock, Inc.; 202 LOC; 203 (l) not available/SS, (c)Glenn Jenkinson/SS, (r) James Steidl/SS; 204 (r) Scott Rothstein/SS, (b) Sandy Felsenthal/Corbis; 205 (b) LOC, (r) GSP Archives; 206 LOC; 207 (l) Scott Rothstein/SS, (r) Underwood & Underwood/Corbis; 208 (t) LOC, (b) Manchester Visual History Collection, Dimond Library, University of New Hampshire; 209 (t) Bill Bernstein/Corbis, (b)The Corcoran Gallery of Art/Corbis; 210 LOC; 211 NHHS; 212 (t) Courtesy of Madeleine Croteau, (bl) LOC, (br) LOC; 213 LOC; 214 Bettmann/ Corbis; 215 (t) Library of Congress, Rare Book and Special Collections Division, (b) Bettman/Corbis; 216 NASA; 217 (t) NASA, (b) Andrea Danti/SS; 218 (r) James M. Phelps, Jr/SS, (l) Lorenzo Mondo/SS; 219 (t) iofoto/SS, (b) Mark Peterson/Corbis; 220 (t) Library of Congress, Prints & Photographs Division, photograph by Tamara Beckwith, (reproduction number, e.g., LC-USZ62-123456), (bl) James Steidl/SS, (br) Carolina K. Smith, M.D./SS; 221 Photo courtesy of the U.S. Army, Photo by Spc. Leslie Angulo; 222 (t) ulga/SS, (b) Ant Clausen/SS; 223 AP Photo/Jim Cole; 224 NASA.

Chapter Ten: 226-227 Joseph Sohm/Visions of America/Corbis; 228 Vladimir Ivanov/SS; 229 (t) National Archives, (b) iStockPhoto/Stefan Klein; 230 CJ Gunther/epa/Corbis; 231 Reuters/Corbis; 233 United States Capitol Historical Society; 234 Associated Press; 235 AP Photo/Jim Cole; 236-237 GSP Archives/ Neal Anderson; 238 Kevin Fleming/Corbis; 239 Darla Hallmark/SS; 240 Jupiter; 241 (t) Courtesy City of Nashua, (b) Dan Habib/Concord Monitor/Corbis; 242-243 GSP Archives/Jon Burton; 244 (t) New Hampshire Division of Travel and Tourism Development(NHDTTD)/Craig Alness, (c) NHDTTD/William Hemmel; 245-246 Joseph Sohm/Visions of America/Corbis; 247 Zack Frank/SS.

Chapter Eleven: 248-249 AP Photo/Larry Crowe; 250 GeoM/SS; 251 (t) michaeljung/SS, (b) PhotoCreate/SS; 252 (bkgrd) not available/SS; 253 (l) Jason Stitt/SS, (b) Marcio Jose Bastos Silva, (r) gary718/SS; 254-255 (l) Denis Selivanov/SS, (b) GSP Archives/Jon Burton, (rt) Valentin Mosichev/SS, spe/SS, (rc) Jupiter, (rb) Yuri Arcurs/SS; 256 Dominique Landau/SS; 258 Jimmy Lee/SS; 259 Anyka/SS; 260 (t) Vedran Vidovic/SS, (bl) GSP Archives/Janis J. Hansen; (br) Courtesy Fuller's Sugar House; 261 (t) Courtesy Peterboro Basket Company, (c) Courtesy Stonyfield Farm, (b) Robyn Mackenzie/SS; 262 (tr) iStockPhoto/Kenneth C. Zirkel, (tc) iStockPhoto/Brent Cebul, (tl) iStockPhoto/Denis Tangney Jr, (cl) iStockPhoto/Kenneth C. Zirkel, (bl) iStockPhoto/Alden Horton, (br) iStockPhoto/Nick Tzolov; 263 (c) Chee-Onn Leong/SS, (br) Jupiter; 264 (c)GSP Archives/Gary Rasmussen, (tl) Morning Goddess/SS, (cl) Jill Battaglia/SS, (bl) Beneda Miroslav/SS, (br) United States Mint; 265 (b) Jupiter, (r) Alexander Kalina/SS; 266 (t) Jupiter, (b) Atanas Bezov/SS; 267 (t) Thank You/SS, (b) Jesse Kunerth/SS; 268 NHHS.